Who's Coming For Dinner

I dedicate this book in loving memory to my
Mother-in-Law
Karen "Kainy" Leslie.

Her enthusiastic spirit first introduced me to
my deep passion and enjoyment for food.
Mealtime was always an interesting event. Her
evident joy in the kitchen was unforgettable.
Believe me when I say, dinner was always an
amazing experience with Karen.
I miss you dearly.

by

Jeffrey W. Suddaby

Photography by Kelly Holinshead

ISBN 0-9735008-0-8

Manufactured in Canada - First Edition

Creative Direction Johanne Stewart

special thanks

Bev, my wife, best friend and best critic. Her depth of knowledge as a Dietitian is a constant and true inspiration. Bev, and my children, Jocelyn and Torin keep my life balanced and complete with their unconditional love and support.

Tamara Marcus, and the supportive people behind Generator Films for taking a dedicated interest in a dream and helping to make it real.

Drew Taylor, for initially putting my recipes together with energy, organization and creativity.

DeVonna Taylor, my personal administrative assistant, for her dynamite writing skills, enthusiasm and dedication towards seeing me meet my many goals.

Kelly Holinshead, for capturing the flavour of my recipes with her creative and talented photography.

Dietitians, Sarah Vogelzang, Mary Ellen Dean & Kim Bendall, who each offered their time, interest and knowledge.

Jack, Judy and Johanne Stewart for spending the time to give this cookbook its artistic flair and design.

Barry Marcus for his administration with the Cookbook.

Mark Soucie of Flotrons Tweed & Hickory and Bev, Carol, Debbie and Joan for all the wrapping and unwrapping of dishware used in photographs. So much tissue paper!

Gerri Mar and DeVonna Taylor for use of dishware from their private collections.

Sandi Munz for making me look good and always being flexible with her schedule.

Randy Robinson, his managers and staff at Independent Grocers for great customer service and support.

Alain Servant, and each member of my staff at 3 Guys & A Stove. To those who create in the kitchen, producing my recipes over and over and to those in the front of the restaurant who represent, 'who I am, and what I strive to be'.

Thanks to all of you, you are truly great and very much appreciated, and I could not have done this cookbook without each and every one of you!

Who's
Coming
For
Dinner

the show

Contents

My culinary journey has allowed me to meet interesting, creative, and hard-working people who want to eat great tasting meals, but can't find the time to prepare an elaborate recipe. This subject came up so often, it inspired me to tell people about the true simplicity of creating delicious food. It is quite easy to turn cooking into an experience and adventure instead of an unpleasant task or chore. A complicated recipe or unrealistic method is completely unnecessary when cooking tasty meals. One of the inspiring truths about cooking is the enormous possibilities that exist when creating a meal. Incredible options are there, from even the simplest of kitchens, and allow anyone to dive into the delicious world of flavour.

Jeff getting ready to tape one of his shows on set

introduction

Lifestyle cuisine, the principle and foundation of my cooking style and this cookbook, was constructed to show people the ease and enjoyment that can be had when cooking flavourful food, while still meeting the demands of today's busy schedules. My purpose with this book is to present an attitude and method for cooking that encourages anyone, from the beginner to the experienced, to use their imagination and explore the endless possibilities of flavour, and to get into the kitchen and have some fun! In these 10 tips I explain the principles behind lifestyle cuisine. By applying these simple recommendations you will find it easier and easier to create and enjoy meals that are loaded with flavour.

1. Make it quick, make it easy and packed full of flavour Don't waste time with elaborate recipes, the shorter the recipe the quicker the meal. Look for recipes that include a lot of herbs and avoid those that use creamy foods on a daily basis. Enjoy richer foods as an occasional treat. We do have to keep in shape.

2. Use staple foods. Keep the cupboards and fridge well stocked with staple foods such as vegetables, herbs and pastas, grains and beans. It is easy to put a meal together with a few fresh vegetables, some stock, a pinch of herbs and pasta or rice.

3. Make healthy choices. Try to reduce high-fat dressings and read the nutritional information on packages to determine the nutritional value of food.

4. When cooking fish, select fresh market fish. Most grocery stores have a fresh fish counter with a variety of fish to choose from. Fish provides a great alternative to meat and poultry.

5. When cooking red meats ensure quality and proper aging. Look at the marbling in the meat. The more marbled the meat the higher the quality. Try to purchase red meats that are dark in colour and not bright red. Aged meat allows the meat to relax and become tender.

6. Always use the freshest vegetables available, although some frozen vegetables are quite acceptable. Even though it's good to have a supply of fresh vegetables, some vegetables are easier to buy frozen, for example, peas and corn. Frozen vegetables can be added quickly to a dish to increase flavour, taste and appearance.

7. Substitute stocks (vegetable, chicken, fish and beef) instead of heavy creams. Adding stock to a recipe will add flavour and is a great alternative to creamier sauces that usually carry extra calories. Canned stocks with no MSG are readily available at your grocers.

8. Don't be scared to cook with spices, add a little sweetness if you need to offset some possible heat, and remember, not all spice is hot. A little curry or some hot peppers can add a nice touch to many foods. If you find you have made a dish too hot don't throw it away, simply add a little sweetness like honey to mellow it out.

9. Mix and match different ethnic cooking procedures, for example cook pasta with a southwestern flair. Try out new combinations. Do not be afraid to combine two recipes, you may be surprised how much you like the different flavours. This gives your cooking a new taste that's exciting and fresh.

10. Last but not least, cook to have fun. Cooking can be a great way to relieve stress and it's instant gratification you can eat! A great deal of satisfaction can be gained from cooking your own tasty meal. The more you cook the more confidence you'll gain and the more compliments you'll receive.

let's shop

LET'S GO SHOPPING

It's quite easy to find the ingredients that you will need to create a sensational and tasty meal. The basic staples required for eating these flavour-filled dishes are usually right around the corner in your local grocery store. There really is no need to find rare and expensive ingredients. Flavour and taste come from imagination and passion, not extravagance and rarity. However, if you find yourself near any local fresh farmers' markets, I would encourage you to pick up a variety of fresh produce, herbs, cheeses, and meat. It's wonderful to have a refrigerator full of options and variety. I've put together a shopping list of some basic herbs, spices, and staples that you can use to get started.

FRESH VERSUS DRIED

If you have the opportunity to purchase fresh herbs, do so, but purchase small amounts in order to achieve continued freshness. Fresh herbs are fragrant and heighten flavour. That being said, it's not always feasible to have fresh herbs on hand, so use dried. The key with using dried spices is shelf life. Generally, dried herbs and ground spices retain their freshness for about 1 year. If your spices are older than that, I recommend you replace them. Fresh pasta is great, but if you only have dried, no worries, life will move on.

SHOPPING FOR THE PANTRY

Vinegar: Balsamic, Rice, White Wine, Red Wine, Cider
Flour: All-purpose, Buckwheat, Whole Wheat
Corn Meal
Cornstarch
Baking Powder
Baking Soda
Couscous, Bulgur
Sugars: Demerara, White and Powdered
Oil: Olive, Citrus Olive, Canola, Sunflower
Soy Sauce
Rice: Arborio, Wild, Multi-grain, Basmati, Brown
Dried Barley
Olives: Kalamata, Green
Fresh Ginger (store unused portion in the freezer, simply zest or chop the amount needed for recipe)
Sun-dried Tomatoes
Dried Pasta: Spaghetti, Penne, Farfalle, Orzo, Rigatoni, Jumbo shells and Fettuccini
Powered or Canned Stocks (no MSG) Vegetable, Beef, Chicken and Fish
Red Pepper Jelly
Horseradish (high-quality)
Mustards: Whole-Grain Dijon, Dry and Dijon
Dried Cranberries, Cherries and Raisins
Nuts: Pecans, Walnuts, Hazelnuts, Cashews, and Almonds

Light canned Coconut Milk
Maple Syrup
Honey
Cinnamon
Whole Nutmeg
Marjoram
Tarragon
Bay Leaves
Poppy Seeds
Sesame Seeds
Sea Salt
Curry powder or Paste: Red and Green
Thyme
Oregano
Basil
Black Pepper
Rosemary
Chilies
Sage
Mint
Seasoned Salts
Mustard Seed
Cajun Seasoning
Fresh Chives
Fresh Parsley

HERE'S THE DIFFERENCE

If you do find yourself using dried herbs instead of fresh simply use half the amount called. For example, if you are preparing a dish that calls for a tablespoon of fresh basil and you can't get your hands on any, no sweat, just substitute half a tablespoon of dried basil. It's that easy!

If you do have the time to make your own stock, your work will be rewarded in the end. When I make a chicken or beef stock I simply save my chicken, steak, and beef bones, and freeze them until I have a freezer bag full. To punch up the flavour, I like to use onions, carrots, celery, Garlic cloves, and several springs of fresh herbs like thyme, marjoram, rosemary, bay leaf, and peppercorns. This is not an exact science. Here are a few of my 'stock tips' to keep in mind; Browning bones and vegetables in the oven before simmering adds colour and flavour to your soup.Once stock has achieved boil reduce heat to a simmer. One of the main things that happens as a meat stock simmers is that gelatin is extracted from the bones, which offers that smooth silkiness in your mouth. After the stock is brought to a boil you may notice a scum floating on the top. Simply skim it off with a slotted spoon and discard. As stock is simmering and reducing, check the pot from time to time giving it a quick stir. The bones will begin to fall apart, and vegetables will break up when the stock is finished. If I have the time I like to strain the stock through a fine-mesh sieve and refrigerate overnight so that I can remove the layer of fat that rises to the surface. When your stock is finished you can use it immediately or freeze it for later use. Its that easy. The following are some of my favorite soup recipes that are sure to please the pallet. Taste, enjoy, and be proud of your creation!

LET'S CHANGE IT UP...

If you are looking for something a little different or don't wish to use cream try using coconut milk in a cream soup. My favourite is seafood chowder with coconut milk, grated chilies and fresh lime, a touch of Thai to a traditional East Coast favorite.

S

soups

SEARED SCALLOP & SWEET COCONUT SOUP

If you are in the mood for an exciting, unique flavour and perhaps even some culinary adventure then this easy Asian soup is a must try. An uncomplicated list of ingredients, with simple instructions makes this soup a great choice, especially since it fits into a busy lifestyle and can be prepared in about 20 minutes. This is pure, sweet enjoyment!

Serves 6

18 Scallops
6 oz dried Rice Noodles
6 cups Fish Stock*
3 cups Coconut Milk (light)
2 teaspoons grated Ginger
1 teaspoon cracked Red Chilies
3 tablespoons Sesame Seeds
Cracked Black Pepper and Salt to taste
1/2 cup fresh Spinach leaves – thinly sliced like ribbons
1 Lime, sliced

Fish Stock

1/2 cup Fish Powder (available on the shelf at your local grocer)
6 cups Water
*Simply bring water to a boil, add powder, and then simmer for 5 minutes.

TIPS

To really speed up the making of this soup, you can reconstitute the stock the day before and wash and drain the spinach, wrap it in a tea towel and store it in a plastic bag. Keep both in the refrigerator until ready to use the next day. You will have an utterly delectable soup in minutes! A simple way to speed up the prep time with this dish is to cook the pasta the day before making sure you shock it with cold water, thoroughly drain and store it in a zipped plastic bag.

Place the noodles in hot water and set aside for 5 minutes, pour into colander, drain and set aside. Heat a pan on high; add Scallops, Sesame Seeds, Ginger, Chilies, and sauté for 2 minutes. Add Stock, Coconut Cream and Lime; simmer for about 6 minutes. Add Noodles, Spinach ribbons and continue simmering for 7 minutes or until tender. Ladle soup into 6 bowls with 3 Scallops per bowl.

SEARED SCALLOP & SWEET COCONUT SOUP

CREAM OF ROASTED ROOT VEGETABLE SOUP

Extremely healthy and multi-layered flavouring would summarize this soup. I quite enjoy the way the root vegetables all flow together, yet hold on to their own individual tastes. This allows you to build layers of flavour for your taste buds to explore. By using the milk in place of cream, you preserve the full-flavoured taste experience while consuming a lighter fare meal.

Serves 6
4 cups of Vegetable Broth
3 medium cloves Garlic, minced
1/2 cup Onions, 1/4" sliced
1/2 cup Carrots, 1/4" sliced
1/2 cup Turnip, 1/4" sliced
1/2 cup Beets, 1/4" sliced
1/2 cup White Radish, 1/4" sliced
1/2 cup Parsnips, 1/4" sliced
4 tablespoons Cilantro Pesto
2 cans of 1% Evaporated Milk
1/4 cup Parsley, chopped
3 Leaves Fresh Basil, chopped
Salt and Pepper to taste

Cilantro Pesto
6 tbsp Garlic
2 tbsp Cumin
2 tsp Paprika
1 tsp Salt
1/2 tsp Cayenne
1/2 tsp Pepper
1 cup Parsley, chopped
1/2 cup Cilantro, chopped
6 tbsp Lemon Juice
4 tbsp Oil

Vegetable Broth
1 cup Vegetable Stock Powder
4 cups Water
Bring water to boil, add powder, and reduce to simmer.

In a medium saucepan, add Oil and heat. Once heated add Garlic, Onions, Carrots, Turnips, Beets, White Radish and Parsnips and sauté for 2 minutes. Add Vegetable Broth and Evaporated Milk and simmer, but make sure you do not boil. Now you can add the Cilantro Pesto, Basil and Parsley. Salt and pepper to your own desired taste. Simmer it all for about 30 minutes.

Simply combine all ingredients in a food processor and blend until smooth. This product is nice because it can be stored in the refrigerator for up to 2 weeks after it is made, and can be used for extra seasoning in many other dishes such as Fish, Lamb, grilled Sausage, Salads, Frittatas and Dressings.

CREAM OF ROASTED ROOT VEGETABLE SOUP

CURRIED SWEET POTATO & PUMPKIN SOUP

Straight from my kitchen to yours, this soup is a taste event you do not want to miss. This is comfort food at its finest and appeals to people of all ages ranging from children to grandparents and everyone in between. You can make it ahead and simply reheat it when you are ready to serve. Your reward will be a great tasting soup and many compliments.

Serves 6

1 tsp Canola Oil
1 tsp Garlic, minced
1 cup Red Onion, finely chopped
4 cups Vegetable Stock (store bought powder or canned stock can be used, preferably no MSG)
1 large Sweet Potato, peeled and chopped
2 cups Pumpkin, cooked and mashed
1 1/2 tsp Curry Powder*
1 tsp Cilantro, chopped plus 5 stems reserved for garnish
3 tbsp Honey
1/4 tsp Ginger, ground
1 cup 2% milk, evaporated

*If you do not have Curry, substitute 3/4 tsp each of cumin and turmeric

Begin by heating a non-stick frying pan, then add your Oil and follow with Onion and Garlic. Sauté the Onion until it becomes transparent, approximately 5 minutes should do the trick. In a separate pot, add the Stock, Sweet Potato, Pumpkin, Curry, Cilantro, Honey and Ginger. Cover and simmer until Potatoes are tender, this should take approximately 40 minutes. Combine the prepared ingredients in a food processor or blender until smooth. At this point in the recipe, meaning before the Milk is added, you can store the soup in your refrigerator for about 4 days or so, which is nice for a dinner party because you can prepare the dish in advance; simplifying your evening. To serve, heat up soup and slowly add enough Milk to achieve desired consistency, about 3/4 cup. I like to serve the soup in heated bowls and garnish with the additional chopped Cilantro, giving the dish the simple and pleasant presentation it deserves.

CURRIED SWEET POTATO & PUMPKIN SOUP

MUSHROOM BARLEY SOUP

This soup is a perfect example of lifestyle cuisine; it is quick and easy, fantastically flavoured, and completely healthy. There is a good chance that most of these ingredients, other that the fresh mushrooms are already in your cupboards or refrigerator. This soup catapults into a new level of deliciousness when you use all three varieties of mushrooms because the better the mushroom, the greater the experience.

Serves 6

6 cups of Vegetable Broth*
1/2 cup Button Mushrooms, washed and sliced
1/2 cup Oyster Mushrooms, washed and sliced
1/2 cup Shiitake Mushrooms, washed and sliced
1 cup Pearl Barley, parboiled**
1 medium Carrot, peeled and diced into 1/4 inch pieces
2 small ribs of Celery, peeled and diced into 1/4 inch pieces
1 tbsp Oil
1 small Onion, minced
3 medium Garlic Cloves, minced
1 tbsp Celery Leaves, coarsely chopped
2 tbsp fresh Dill, coarsely chopped
Salt and fresh Ground Black Pepper, to taste

Vegetable Broth

1 cup Vegetable Stock Powder
4 cups Water
Bring water to boil, add powder, and reduce to simmer.

TIPS

**Parboil Pour 1 cup of pearl barley into 2 cups of salted rapidly boiling water. Add the Barley in quantities so that the boiling process is not disturbed. Boil until Barley has absorbed the liquid and is just tender. Place Barley in a colander and set aside until recipe calls for it.

Heat a medium to large saucepan, add Oil, Carrots, Celery, Garlic, Onions, sauté for 2 minutes. Add all of the Mushrooms and sauté for an additional 2 minutes. Pour in the Vegetable Broth and add the cooked Barley, Celery Leaves and Dill. Salt and Pepper to your own desired taste. Simmer for about 30 minutes and serve hot.

MUSHROOM BARLEY SOUP

BEEF AND ROASTED
VEGETABLE & HORSERADISH SOUP

The addition of horseradish with its pungent scent and spicy zing is the perfect compliment to this rich beef and hearty vegetable soup.

Serves 6

12 oz Beef, diced and trimmed of fat, outside round or a cut of your choice
2 cups of the following vegetables:
    Turnip, cut into matchsticks
    Onion, sliced
    Carrots, cut into matchsticks
    Mushrooms, quartered
    Red, Green and Orange Peppers, cut into matchsticks
    Eggplant, cut into matchsticks
30 oz Demi-glaze,* or Beef Stock
2 cloves Garlic, minced
3 tbsp Olive Oil
1 tsp dried Basil
1/2 tsp dried Oregano
8 sprigs fresh Rosemary
Fresh Black Cracked Pepper

I prefer Demi-glaze because of its rich flavour and texture, but you may substitute beef stock
When using any prepared stock or Demi-glaze it is usually not necessary to add salt, since there is already salt in the powder.
Fresh Horseradish is divine, simply grate the root, add a teaspoon of Vinegar, a tablespoon or two of Sour Cream, Yogurt or Mayonnaise, Salt and Pepper to taste.

Make Demi-glaze according to instructions on package, set aside. Heat a large pan to medium-high, add Oil and sear Beef to a golden brown. Add Vegetable mixture, dried herbs and Garlic and sauté until Onions becomes transparent. Add prepared Demi-glaze and 2 sprigs of Rosemary and bring to a boil, immediately reducing heat and simmering for 1 hour. Add Black Cracked Pepper to taste. To serve, place soup in 6 bowls, place 1 sprig of Rosemary and 1 tsp of Horseradish on top of each soup.

BEEF AND ROASTED VEGETABLE & HORSERADISH SOUP

CHICKEN & RICE PASTA SOUP

Variations on chicken soup are endless, so here is my version of a soup made in every country. I find making and eating chicken soup therapeutic with its inviting fragrance and hearty, chocked full of flavour taste. You may ask if chicken soup is a cure and I say, who cares...it is delicious!

Serves 6

8 oz boneless Chicken Breast (you may use any chicken meat)
48 oz Chicken Stock (may use powdered and reconstitute with water or a quality canned)
1 Onion, sliced
2 cloves Garlic, minced
3 tbsp Olive Oil
1+ 1/2 tsp dried Basil
1/2 tsp + 1/4 tsp dried Oregano
1/2 cup raw Orzo pasta, cooked al denté, shocked and drained
3 stalks Celery, diced
3 Carrots, diced
2 sprig fresh Sage or 1/2 tsp dried
2 tbsp Soya Sauce
1/2 cup Turnip, cut into matchsticks
1/2 cup Red and Orange Peppers, cut into matchsticks
6 sprigs Cilantro to garnish

TIPS

The Orzo Pasta will heat simply by adding the hot soup.

Heat skillet on medium-high, add half the Oil, sauté Chicken Breast on both sides with 1/2 tsp Basil and 1/4 tsp Oregano; remove Chicken to a side plate and hold. Deglaze skillet with half cup of stock, scraping bottom of pan to loosen any bits of flavour. Remove skillet from heat and set aside. Heat a soup pan to medium-high, add the other half of Oil, Garlic, Onions, Carrot, Turnip, fresh Sage and sauté until Onions become transparent. Dice Chicken and add to soup pan. Add the stock you used to deglaze skillet, and all other stock, Soya Sauce and the rest of the herbs. Bring to a boil, reduce heat to a simmer, until Chicken is thoroughly cooked. Divide cooked pasta into six bowls. Pour soup into each bowl. Garnish with Cilantro.

CHICKEN & RICE PASTA SOUP

BLACK BEAN & CORN CHOWDER

This one-pot unpretentious dish soothes and satisfies even the hungriest of eaters. Treat your taste buds and your body to this flavourful and filling soup.

Serves 6

3/4 cup Black Beans* (may use canned, un-drained)
3/4 cup Corn, fresh or frozen
1 Onion, diced
1 tsp dried Basil
1/2 tsp dried Oregano
3/4 cup Potatoes, diced
3 stalks Celery, diced
3 Carrots, diced
24 oz of the following liquid:
   Either half milk and half vegetable stock** (may use quality canned)
   Or
   One fourth 35% Cream and three-quarters vegetable stock
1/4 pound Butter
1/4 cup Flour
2 Bay Leaves
Fresh cracked Black Pepper to taste

TIPS

Chowder is better when allowed to 'cure' for at least one hour and even up to three days, allowing the flavours to blend, which heightens and intensifies the taste. Chowder can taste great made with seafood, and almost any type of vegetable. Any chowder, milk- or broth-based, will have a richer body and taste if you increase the volume and variety of vegetables. This is especially true with vegetables that are starchy, like potatoes, corn and beans.

Heat a skillet to medium-high, add Butter, Potatoes, Onions, Celery, Carrot, and Herbs sautéing until Onions become transparent. Sprinkle Flour, stirring to coat vegetable mixture; slowly add stock and cream mixture, stirring constantly creating a roux-like mixture. Add Corn, Beans and simmer 30 minutes or until Potatoes are thoroughly cooked. Add fresh cracked Black Pepper to taste.

*To cook Beans, take 3/4 cup dried Black Beans, 1 - 1/2 cups Water, 1-teaspoon Salt, put in large saucepan and bring to a boil, then simmer until beans are thoroughly cooked.

**You may notice I have not called for the addition of Salt and that is because there is Salt in the prepared vegetable stock. The purpose of Salt is to bring out all the flavour of the food, not for the food to taste salty.

BLACK BEAN & CORN CHOWDER

MUSSEL, SCALLOP & TIGER SHRIMP BROTH

This dish from the sea offers a plethora of flavour, from the sweetness of scallops to the juiciness of mussels and the mega flavour of the shrimps, all enhanced with garlic, herbs and the added dimension of white wine making this broth a delicious gift from the ocean.

Serves 6
24 large Shrimp, peeled and deveined
6 Scallops
18 Mussels, rinsed
3 Garlic Cloves, minced
2 tbsp Olive Oil
2 tsp dried Basil
1 tsp dried Oregano
36 oz Fish Stock, (can use powder, reconstituted with water)
12 Lime, slices
6 Cilantro Flowers, fresh
1/2 cup White Wine (use a quality you would drink)
12 Chive stems

TIPS

I like to put an empty bowl on the table for Mussel shells. The broth is great with warm Baguette or Rolls.

Heat a pan to medium-high; add Oil, Scallops, Shrimp, Mussels and Garlic sautéing until Shrimps turn colour, approximately 2-3 minutes. Deglaze with White wine and reduce liquid by half. Add Herbs, Stock and Limes, bringing liquid to a simmer, cooking 3-5 minutes longer. Serve in big bowls, garnishing each bowl with 2 Chive stems and Limes

MUSSEL, SCALLOP & TIGER SHRIMP BROTH

There are enormous varieties when it comes to making salads and salad dressings. Many great recipes come from culinary exploration and imagination, for example, the use of oil in a salad is not always necessary, instead try using flavored vinegars, honey, or your favorite fruit juice in place of oil, these can perk up a salad with a burst of flavour. Explore different greens, vegetables, and fruits and incorporate flavour enhancers like mustard seeds, poppy seeds, or sesame seeds. Choices are endless and your salads will come alive. Great discovery usually comes from continued exploration so here's a thought; try to incorporate a new green, vegetable, or homemade dressing into your salads at least once a week. There's a whole new world of taste waiting for you!

When making a salad I would suggest using a varied mixture of hard and soft vegetables; a good balance between these two will make any salad more interesting. Of course the fresher your ingredients the more intense the flavour, so if you have the chance to stop by a market or even the side of the road to pick up some fresh produce. I encourage you to do so. However, if you find that your selection comes from your local supermarket then get the best quality you can find, great taste will still be there.

HEY! LISTEN TO THIS...

Sometimes I like to use a salad dressing as a base for a different recipe. Experiment by adding a little of this and that, and you can create an outstanding dressing. It's a great way to add a little personalized flair to your salad. Explore the choices!

salads

BLACK BEAN GARDEN SALAD
WITH RASPBERRY APRICOT VINAIGRETTE

I made this salad with comedian Wade McElwain on my television cooking show, *Who's Coming For Dinner*. We had fun making and eating it and I think you will too. The colour, texture and taste sensation is like no other and is sure to please most anyone's pallet.

Serves 6
3/4 cup Black Beans, cooked
1/3 cup Red Bell Pepper, seeded and chopped
1/3 cup Yellow Bell Pepper, seeded and chopped
3/4 cup Cucumber, peeled, seeded and cubed
3/4 cup medium Red Onion, sliced into half rounds
2 Tomatoes, seeded and chopped
3/4 cup Fresh Cilantro, chopped
6 large leaves Red Leaf Lettuce, chilled
Snipped Fresh Chives, for garnish

Raspberry Apricot Vinaigrette
1 tsp Dijon Mustard
2 tsp Raspberry Vinegar
1/2 cup Apricot Nectar
1/4 tsp Red Pepper Flakes, crushed
3 tbsp Canola Oil
Salt and Pepper to taste

Wade McElwain

Combine the Black Beans, Vegetables and Cilantro in a large salad bowl and mix well. Prepare the Vinaigrette by simply mixing all the ingredients together in a small bowl with a whisk. Pour the dressing over the Bean and Vegetable mixture and toss thoroughly. Cover and chill for at least 1 hour before serving. When I make this salad for guests I like to put the salad plates that I am going to use in the refrigerator to chill. When you are ready to serve, line each plate with chilled Leaf Lettuce, and top with a serving of Bean Salad. By using the snipped Chives for a garnish and serving your salad in chilled bowls you can add an element of simple elegance to your style.

BLACK BEAN GARDEN SALAD WITH RASPBERRY APRICOT VINAIGRETTE

ENDIVE & WATERMELON
WITH LEMON MINT MANGO VINAIGRETTE

I took one of my favourite salad greens, Endive, and combined it with one of my favourite cheeses Feta and thought, why not add one of my favourite fruits which is Watermelon...but I couldn't stop...I added a bit of Lemon Mint and then drizzled one very flavourful Mango Dressing over the whole thing. *Oh,...I'm here to tell you, life is good!*

Serves 6
6 cups Endive
6 cups Watermelon, cubed
6 oz Feta Cheese, low-fat
6 leaves of Lemon Mint

Mango Vinegar Dressing
2 oz Mango Vinegar
1 tbsp Orange Juice
1 tbsp Lime Juice
1/4 tsp Sugar
1/4 tsp Dijon Mustard

Whisk together the above ingredients in a small bowl and drizzle over each plate of greens.

TIPS

If Endive is too strong for your taste, try Mixed Greens or Spinach. If you cannot locate Mango Vinegar, use another fruit-based Vinegar like Berry or Pear. To heighten the flavour even more, zest some Citrus peel into the dressing.

Make Mango Dressing and set aside
Wash and dry Endive, put on 6 plates
Cut Watermelon into 1 inch cubes, put 1 cup over Endive on each plate
Crumble 1 oz Feta Cheese over each plate
Pour Mango Vinegar Dressing over each Salad (See recipe above)
Garnish with Lemon Mint

ENDIVE & WATERMELON WITH LEMON MINT MANGO VINAIGRETTE

CUCUMBER AND TOMATO
WITH FETA & RED WINE VINAIGRETTE

Do not let the simplicity of this salad fool you. Packed with flavour, this quick, hassle-free dish allows you to eat great tasting food without wasting time on an elaborate recipe. It is a nice little variation for all the Greek salad lovers out there.

Serves 6
4 Tomatoes, halved and quartered
2 Cucumbers, halved lengthwise and sliced thickly
1 cup flat leaf Parsley Leaves, chopped
1/4 cup Mint Leaves, halved lengthwise
1 cup of Black Olives, sliced
8 oz Feta Cheese, chopped
Fresh ground Black Pepper
6 Lemon wedges

Dressing
2 tbsp Olive Oil
1 tbsp Red Wine Vinegar
Sea Salt and Fresh Ground Pepper

Prepare the dressing by whisking the Olive Oil, Vinegar, Salt and Pepper; set aside. Place the Tomatoes, Cucumber, Parsley, Mint and Olives in a serving bowl and pour over the dressing. Sprinkle salad with the Feta Cheese and Sea Salt and fresh ground Black Pepper to taste. The Lemon wedges make an excellent garnish. It is as easy as that.

CUCUMBER AND TOMATO WITH FETA & RED WINE VINAIGRETTE

MIXED KITCHEN SALAD
WITH HONEY POPPY SEED DRESSING

Don't let the simple name, Kitchen Salad fool you…it's right out of my kitchen at *3 Guys & A Stove* and is a favourite salad selection. Tantalize your taste buds with the oil-free Poppy Seed Dressing, which can be used successfully on many different salads of your choice.

Serves 4

Lettuce Mix to yield 4 cups (Boston, Chicory, Radicchio, Endive, Red or Green Leaf)
2 cups Romaine lettuce, washed, dried and torn into bit size pieces
8 Tomato slices
8 Red Onion slices
12 oz Chick Peas, rinsed and drained
4 Radishes, quartered
8 Cucumber slices
4 stems of Cilantro, washed
8 Chive stems
1 pinch dried Oregano
2 pinches dried Basil - combine both dried herbs and set aside
4 oz Poppy Seed Dressing (See recipe below)

Poppy Seed Dressing

1/4 cup Rice Vinegar
1 1/2 tsp Poppy Seeds
1 tsp Dijon mustard
2 - 2 1/2 tbsp liquid Honey

For the Poppy Seed Dressing, mix all ingredients together in a small bowl with a whisk. In a large bowl, combine Lettuce Mixture, Onion, Radishes, Chickpeas and Poppy Seed Dressing. Using kitchen tongs, divide salad evenly onto 4 plates. Garnish each plate with even amounts of Tomato, Cucumber and Chives. I like to sprinkle the Dried Herb Mix around the rim of the plate for an extra element of presentation.

MIXED KITCHEN SALAD WITH HONEY POPPY SEED DRESSING

PAPAYA AND WATERCRESS
WITH RASPBERRY WHEAT HONEY & GINGER DRESSING

This salad has what I like to call 'layers of flavour'. First there is the sweet juicy taste of Papaya combined with the peppery flavour of Watercress, drizzled with a zip of citrus, a hint of sweet in the Honey and Apple Juice, followed with the crispness of Mint and the scent of Raspberry Beer. Do you see why I call this 'layers of flavour'?

Serves 4

6 cups Watercress, washed and dried
1 Papaya, large, cleaned and cut into strips
1/2 Red Onion, julienne cut

Combine ingredients in large salad bowl, set aside and make dressing.

Dressing

1/4 cup Honey
1 tsp Ginger, freshly grated
2 oz Apple Juice
1/2 Lemon, juiced
2 tsp Mint, freshly chopped
1/4 cup Raspberry Wheat Beer
Fresh cracked Black Pepper to taste

Put all ingredients into a bowl and whisk thoroughly. Drizzle over salad greens.

TIPS

Papayas will be best if ripened at room temperature. Ripe fruit will keep in the refrigerator up to a week. If an entire salad of Watercress is too much for you, try combining it with your favourite greens.

PAPAYA AND WATERCRESS WITH RASPBERRY WHEAT HONEY & GINGER DRESSING

MIXED GREENS WITH BALSAMIC & OIL
WITH BAKED BAGUETTE

This salad is served 'upside-down'. The mix of leafy greens and crisp Romaine lettuce offers a nice refreshing flavour. What's unique about this salad is that you dip the greens into the dressing instead of pouring the dressing over the salad. Be sure to dip the baguette, it's outstanding. This salad is dynamite with your favourite rice or pasta dish.

Serves 6
3 cups of Mixed Greens
1 cup Romaine lettuce, chopped
12 Cherry Tomatoes
1/4 cup Alfalfa Sprouts
6 leaves fresh Basil, for garnish
24 Baguette slices, cut on the diagonal

Dressing
4 oz Balsamic Vinegar
2 oz Olive Oil
Salt and Pepper to taste

Preheat oven to 400 F. Slice Baguette and bake 7 minutes or until golden brown. Mix all ingredients into a large serving bowl. On 6 individual salad plates, first pour the Oil followed with the Balsamic Vinegar. Vinegar will 'teardrop' in the oil. Place Mixed Greens on top of the Dressing, add Baguette and serve.

MIXED GREENS WITH BALSAMIC & OIL WITH BAKED BAGUETTE

ROASTED MARINATED MUSHROOM SALAD

This is a great treat for the mushroom lovers out there. The Port Wine Vinegar and Feta Cheese meet together to form an exploding taste sensation. If you find these Mushrooms are unavailable or do not make your favorites list, you can easily substitute what you like or what you can get. *Enjoy!*

Serves 6

8 oz Button Mushrooms
8 oz Shiitake Mushrooms
3 oz Enoki Mushrooms
2 tsp Canola Oil
2 - 3 Garlic cloves, minced
6 oz Feta cheese, low-fat
6 oz Port Wine Vinegar
Pinch Oregano
Pinch Basil
7-8 cups of Mixed Greens of your choice, washed and dried

TIPS

Most grocery stores now stock a wide variety of mushrooms. Avoid those that are shriveled or bruised. Here is a quick description of a few of my favourite mushrooms. Some mushrooms are available dried or dehydrated and you just reconstitute with hot water.

Enoki: A delicate tiny cap on a long thin stem and is excellent raw in salads and soups.

Shiitake: Offers an intense, rich woodsy flavour and has a meat like texture. It has the reputation of being the fragrant mushroom.

Portabello: Very hearty in flavour and usually very big, so much so you can grill the tops and make a vegetable 'burger'! They are delicious in many dishes

Italian Brown: About the size of button mushrooms, they have a rich flavour and tender texture

Oyster: These range in colour from off white to brown. This variety produces a better flavour when cooked

Preheat the oven to 450°F

On high heat, in an oven-safe, non-stick skillet put Oil, Garlic, Mushrooms, (Button and Shiitake only), Basil and Oregano; stir to coat mushrooms with Oil and herbs. Roast in oven for 9 minutes. Using oven mitts, remove skillet from oven and deglaze by pouring Port Wine Vinegar over the Mushrooms, scraping the bottom of the pan to loosen any Mushrooms and Herbs. After deglazing, put skillet back into the oven for one more minute. Place Mixed Greens onto 6 plates and pour roasted Mushrooms over the greens followed by the Enoki mushrooms. Garnish with Feta Cheese and Chives.

ROASTED MARINATED MUSHROOM SALAD

ROASTED VEGETABLE SALAD

This warm salad has a rainbow blend of red, green, yellow and purple vegetables and glistens with both flavour and colour. Sweet Basil and Oregano give hints of the Mediterranean.

Serves 2

2 tsp Olive Oil
1/4 tsp Sweet Basil, dried
1/8 tsp Oregano, dried
2 cloves of Garlic, crushed
Pinch Salt
Fresh Black Cracked Pepper

Roasted Vegetable Mixture

2 cups of Lettuce Mixture:*
1/2 Red Onion, sliced thinly
1 Zucchini, cut into quarters lengthwise and diced
1/8 each Green, Red and Yellow Peppers, cored, cut into 1/4 inch strips and chopped
1/3 cup Mushrooms, cut into quarters
1/3 cup Turnip, julienne 1/2 inch thick
1/3 cup Eggplant, cut into 1/2 inch slices and diced
1/4 cup Balsamic Vinegar

TIPS

Be flexible and experiment: If you find that your refrigerator is full of vegetables but they are not those listed above, simply use what you have, or like instead. You will not be jeopardizing the flavour merely tuning it to your needs or desires. If you want to turn this salad into a more hardy lunch, place a sliced, grilled chicken breast on top of the vegetables.

Place 2 salad plates in the freezer to chill. Preheat oven to 450°F

In a roasting pan, thoroughly combine 2 tsp Olive Oil, Vegetable Mixture, Basil, Oregano, Garlic, and Salt. Roast in 450°F oven for about 9 minutes. Next, pour the Balsamic Vinegar over roasted vegetables. Stir the Vinegar with the Vegetable Mixture — scrapping any food stuck to the bottom of the roasting pan. Place the mixture back into the 450°F oven for 2 – 5 minutes or until vegetables crisp without overcooking. Remove plates from freezer, place 1/2 of Romaine Lettuce, and 1 cup Spring Mix into each of the chilled salad plates. Pour grilled Vegetables over Lettuce Mixture. Garnish each salad with 1 Lemon slice, 1 Lime slice and 1 Cilantro flower. Serve immediately with Cracked Pepper.

*Lettuce Mixture:

1/4 Romaine, washed, dried and torn into bite size pieces
2 cups "Spring Mix" (Chicory, Bib, Radicchio, Endive, Red and Green Leaf)
2 Lemon slices
2 Lime slices
4 Chives
2 stems Cilantro

ROASTED VEGETABLE SALAD

SPINACH WITH FRESH STRAWBERRIES, ALMONDS & MAPLE VINAIGRETTE

This salad is as good to eat as it looks, packed with colour, texture and flavour. The delicate Baby Spinach and the crisp Mixed Greens are a perfect base for the crunchy Almonds, mild Red Onion and refreshing fruit, especially when you finish with Maple Vinaigrette. So simple, so easy, so good.

Serves 6

3 cups Baby Spinach
3 cups Mixed Salad Greens
6 tbsp slivered Almonds, toasted to a golden brown
6 tbsp Sun-dried Cranberries
12 fresh Strawberries cut into 4 pieces each (if berries are small, cut in half)
1 Red Onion, sliced thin
1 cup Shiitake Mushrooms, sliced thin

Vinaigrette

1/4 cup Cider Vinegar
2 tbsp Maple Syrup
1 tsp dried Basil
1/2 tsp dried Oregano

Whisk Vinaigrette; set aside.
Combine all the salad ingredients, put in salad bowls or on plates, and drizzle with vinaigrette.

SPINACH WITH FRESH STRAWBERRIES, ALMONDS & MAPLE VINAIGRETTE

TOMATO, ARUGULA, WHITE BEAN & RED ONION WITH HERB GINGER VINAIGRETTE

I love the unique peppery taste that Arugula has to offer, and when mixed with the fresh Ginger, Rice Vinegar, and Soy Sauce your taste buds are in for an intense dance. This aromatic recipe is a great way to add some flare to the salad scene.

Serves 6
4 medium Tomatoes, cut into wedges
1 bunch Arugula, washed and drained (can substitute spinach, mixed greens, etc.)
1/2 Red Onion, sliced into paper thin slices and separated into rings
1 cup canned White Beans, drained and rinsed

Vinaigrette
2 tbsp Rice Vinegar
1 tbsp each; Soy Sauce, fresh Lemon Juice and Olive Oil
2 tsp Sugar
1 clove Garlic, minced
1 tbsp Ginger*, freshly grated or 1/2 tsp of Powder
2 tbsp each chopped fresh Basil and Cilantro

TIPS

Ginger not used may be stored in a freezer bag in the freezer for later use.

In a salad bowl or platter, toss Tomatoes, Arugula, White Beans, and Onion rings. To prepare the vinaigrette simply pour all ingredients into a bowl and whisk together. To finish, pour vinaigrette over salad and serve.

TOMATO, ARUGULA, WHITE BEAN & RED ONION WITH HERB GINGER VINAIGRETTE

YUCATAN PENINSULA CAESAR SALAD

This Caesar Salad recipe instantly became a favourite at *3 Guys & A Stove*. I like to use Jalapeno Peppers because they heighten the flavour of the Garlic.

Serves 6

1 Egg yoke (See tip below)
3 cloves Garlic, minced
1 tbs Dijon Mustard
1 oz Anchovies*
2 oz Worcestershire
1/4 cup Olive Oil
1/2 cup Water
1 Jalapeno (Remove stem, use entire pepper - thoroughly wash hands after cutting)
1 Lemon (the juice)
Salt and fresh Black Cracked Pepper to taste
4 per salad Croutons (homemade is great, but there are excellent store bought choices)
2 heads Romaine Lettuce, washed & dried
3 oz fresh Parmesan Cheese, grated

*If you find using a can of Anchovies messy, try a tube of anchovy paste found at your local grocers. Once opened, keep it stored in the refrigerator. Enjoy the heightened flavour, perhaps even keeping the 'mystery' ingredient a secret from your family.

TIPS

I like to use raw eggs in my caesar salads and I use fresh, clean, refrigerated, uncracked and unbroken Grade "A" Eggs and make my dressing immediately before serving it. Nevertheless, I am aware of the possible risk of salmonella, especially in young children, the elderly and those with compromised immune systems. You will need to make your own decision about using or not using raw Eggs, they can be omitted According to Public health, an egg must reach the internal temperature of 60°C to be completely safe.

Preheat oven 400°F

To make dressing roast Garlic Cloves with skin on in the oven for 5-7 minutes. Remove from oven and cool enough to touch. Peel skin off (many times the bud will pop out by squeezing with fingers). Place the peeled Garlic in blender or food processor with Anchovies, Jalapeno, Egg yoke, Dijon mustard, Worcestershire, Lemon Juice and water. Blend thoroughly; while blender is still on add Oil and continue to blend until desired thickness. Cut or tear Lettuce into a nice-sized salad bowl. Add Croutons, Parmesan Cheese and Dressing, tossing until the Lettuce is coated. Add Salt and Pepper to taste and serve immediately.

Appetizer to Entrée
This salad can be a great lunch or even light dinner entrée simply by adding a grilled, or cajun Chicken Breast on top. *The possibilities are infinite!*

YUCATAN PENINSULA CAESAR SALAD

Pasta is a highly satisfying comfort food and a great staple. Its versatility and flexibility make it a great choice for lifestyle cuisine. Fresh pasta is absolutely the best, so if you can get your hands on some, do so, but don't worry if you can't because great tasting dried pasta can be cooked in minutes, and still offers brilliant taste. I like to prepare my pasta al denté because there is nothing worse than a great sauce and mushy pasta, it just doesn't do the dish justice. When I cook fresh pasta, I like to keep things simple and quick. First add water to a saucepan and bring to a rolling boil. Don't add oil to the water because it 'coats' the pasta and when you add your sauce, it will just slide off. Next add the pasta to the boiling water and cover, this allows the water to recover back to the boil faster. Once the boil returns, cook for another 2 minutes. Always remember, you need to double the volume of water compared to the weight of pasta. For example - to cook 8 oz of pasta, you will need 16 oz of water.

TRY SOMETHING NEW...

Not sure how to cook fresh pasta? The only difference between cooking fresh pasta and dried pasta is the cooking time. The very same rules apply for fresh pasta; once the water is boiling and you add the pasta, cook about 2-3 minutes. The results are magnificent. Treat yourself!

pasta

FARFALLE WITH ROASTED VEGETABLES
& HERB CHICKEN

I prepared this dish with an assist from former NHL player Kris King on *Who's Coming For Dinner*. The goal was to take a simple recipe that shoots for excellent results and has all-star flavour! We scored on this one; it is truly a top-shelf dish.

Serves 6
2-3 Garlic Cloves, minced
2 tbsp Olive Oil
1/2 tbsp Oregano, dried
1 tbsp Basil, dried
6-8 cups Farfalle Pasta, cooked, shocked and drained
12 oz Chicken Breast, boneless and skinned
1/4 of Turnip, chopped
1 Red Onion, chopped
1 cup Mushrooms, quartered
1/2 Red Pepper, chopped
1/4 Yellow Pepper, chopped
1/4 Green Pepper, chopped
1 Zucchini, chopped
2 Tomatoes, diced
1 1/2 cups Chicken Stock (can use powder, reconstituted with Water)
Salt and cracked Black Pepper to taste
12 Chives
6 sprigs Cilantro, washed
6 tbsp Parmesan Cheese, grated

Kris King

Precook the Chicken Breasts and thinly slice. Heat large skillet on medium-high heat. Add Oil, Vegetables, Garlic and Herbs. Sauté until Garlic is golden. Deglaze skillet by pouring 1 cup of stock in skillet and scrape pan with flat spatula to loosen any browning in bottom of skillet. This imparts great flavour to your dish. Add remaining Stock, Pasta, Salt and Pepper. Cook until stock is absorbed. Add Tomatoes just before dish is ready to serve. Plate Farfalle into 6 bowls and garnish with Cilantro and Chives. To finish, I like to grate fresh Parmesan Cheese over each dish.

FARFALLE WITH ROASTED VEGETABLES & HERB CHICKEN

FETTUCCINE WITH TOMATO, BASIL & OLIVE

This is a great dish if you're looking for a quick and easy pasta solution. I like to use Fettuccine but as always feel free to substitute what you have or desire. The hint of Sugar in this recipe adds the perfect level of sweetness, leaving your mouth wanting more with each bite.

Serves 6
1 1/2 lb. cooked Fettuccine
1 1/2 tbsp Olive Oil
1 1/2 Onion, chopped
3 Garlic Cloves, crushed
3 large Tomatoes, chopped
1/2 cup fresh Basil, chopped
1/4 cup Black Olives, sliced
Cracked Black Pepper and Sea Salt
Pinch Demerera Sugar
6 oz Parmesan Cheese
3 cups vegetable Stock
1 tps chilies

In a large frying pan on medium heat add the Oil, Onion and Garlic and cook for 4 minutes or until lightly golden. Add the Tomatoes, and simmer for another 4 minutes. Stir in Basil, Olives, Chilies, Pepper, Salt and Sugar. To finish, toss the sauce with pasta, top with Parmesan Cheese and serve.

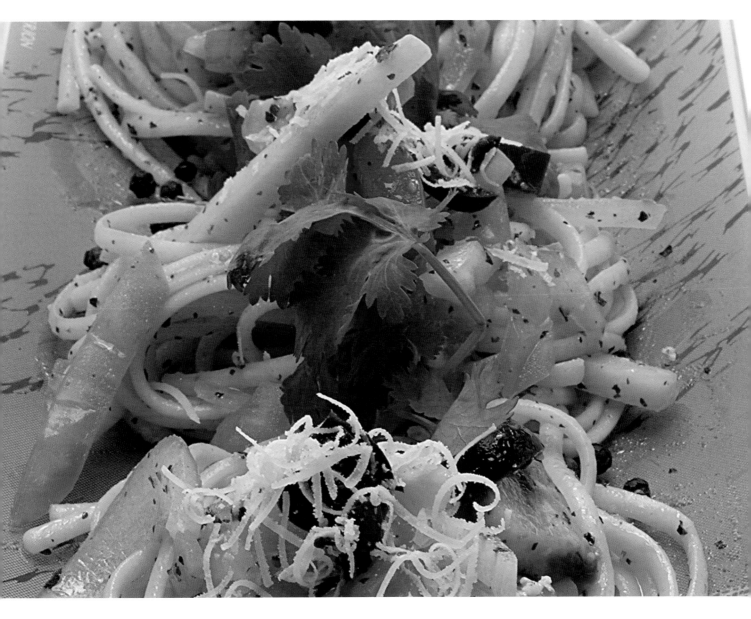

FETTUCCINE WITH TOMATO, BASIL & OLIVE

SEAFOOD ORZO

I like to use Alaska Scallops with this dish, but if you need to use up something from your refrigerator or freezer, or you are not in the mood for scallops, you can easily replace them with Alaska Cod, Pollock, Sole, Flounder or Halibut fillets. Any of these choices are incredibly delicious with this recipe. I love the Dill, Feta, and Artichoke combination and I am betting your taste buds with scream for more.

Serves 6
6 sheets of foil (12 inches each off the roll)
6 sheets Parchment Paper
1 1/2 pound raw Alaska Scallops
4 1/2 cups Orzo Pasta, cooked, shocked and drained
1 1/2 can Artichoke Hearts, drained and quartered
3 cups Cherry Tomato, halved
3 Garlic Cloves, minced
Juice of 1-1/2 Lemons
3 tbsp Olive Oil
Salt and freshly Ground Pepper
4 tbsp chopped fresh Dill or 2 tablespoons dried Dill Weed
2 ounces Feta Cheese, low-fat
Lemon and Lime slices to garnish

TIPS

This can be made on the BBQ

Preheat oven to 375°F or grill to medium high.
In a large bowl, combine Orzo, Artichokes, Cherry Tomatoes, Garlic, Lemon Juice, Olive Oil, Salt, Pepper, and Dill. Center one sixth of Orzo mixture on each sheet of foil, place fish over orzo mixture. Bring all four corners up to meet, crimp foil to make a "package", leaving room for heat circulation inside. Repeat to make six packages. Bake 14-18 minutes on a cookie sheet (or grill 9-11 minutes in a covered grill). Remove each package and place on individual plates. Open package and slide mixture off foil. Sprinkle with Feta Cheese. Garnish with Lemon and Lime slices

SEAFOOD ORZO

SPICY PENNE WITH WHITE BEANS

Another great dish made with the help of former NHL player Kris King. This time we decided to heat things up in the second period. The Sundried Tomatoes and white beans are an excellent and tasty combination, and when topped with Feta Cheese, which helps cut the heat, each bite will melt in your mouth. This dish can be zingy with spice or mellow and mild, because just like the referee in hockey, it is the chef here who makes that call.

Serves 6

2-3 Garlic Cloves, minced
2 tbsp Olive Oil
1/2 tbsp Oregano, dried
1 tbsp Basil, dried
2 Tomatoes, diced
1/4 of Turnip, chopped
1 Red Onion, chopped
1/4 cups Button Mushrooms, quartered
1/2 Red pepper, chopped
1/4 Yellow pepper, chopped
1/4 Green pepper, chopped
1 Zucchini, chopped
12 oz White Cooked Beans (rinse and drain if using canned)
6 tbsp Sundried Tomato mix (can be purchased at grocers)
4 oz White Wine (not cooking wine), mix with 4-oz water
1 1/2 cups Vegetable Stock
3 cups Penne Pasta, cooked, shocked and drained
12 oz Black Olives, sliced
18 oz Feta Cheese, crumbled in chunks
Red Chili Peppers to taste
Salt to taste
6 flowers of Cilantro, washed
12 Chives
6-8 tbsp fresh Parmesan Cheese, grated

Heat a large skillet on medium-high heat; add Oil, Vegetables, Garlic, Vegetable Stock, and Herbs. Sauté 1-2 minutes. Add Sundried Tomatoes and Olives and sauté 1-2 minutes longer. Deglaze skillet by pouring wine mixture in skillet and scrape pan with flat spatula to loosen any browning in bottom of skillet. This imparts flavour. Add Stock, Beans, Pasta, Chilies and Salt. Cook until Stock is absorbed. Add Tomatoes just before the dish is ready to serve. Plate Penne into 6 bowls and garnish with Feta, Cilantro and Chives. Grate fresh Parmesan Cheese over each dish.

SPICY PENNE WITH WHITE BEANS

PASTA SHELLS STUFFED WITH SPINACH RICOTTA, COTTAGE CHEESE & FRESH TOMATOES

Mamma Mia! These rich and creamy stuffed Pasta Shells, covered with a colourful medley of roasted Vegetables and mild and smokey Provolone Cheese are bound to please anyone of any age.

Serves 4

20 large Pasta Shells
2 cups fresh Spinach, washed, dried and cut into ribbons
1 cup Ricotta Cheese
1 cup Cottage Cheese
2 tbsp Walnuts, chopped
1 tsp Basil, dried
1/2 tsp Oregano, dried
Sea Salt and cracked Pepper, to taste
2 large Plum Tomatoes, diced
6 oz Tomato Juice
2 tbsp fresh Parsley, roughly chopped
1 cup Olive Oil
1 tbsp Brown Sugar
1/4 of a Turnip, cut into matchsticks
1/2 of an Onion, cut into matchsticks
1 Beet, peeled and cut into matchsticks
2 Garlic Cloves, minced
10 oz Provolone Cheese, cut into 20 slices that are about the size of a 'toonie' each

TIPS

Use disposable rubber gloves to avoid staining your hands when working with Beets.

Preheat oven 400°F

Cook Pasta Shells in boiling water to an al denté stage, drain, shock in cold water, drain again, and set aside. In a food processor, blend Ricotta & Cottage Cheese, Spinach, Salt and Pepper. Remove from processor; add Walnuts and stir. Stuff shells with the cheese mixture, placing them seam side up in a baking dish. Heat a Skillet over med-high, add 1-3 tbsp Oil; sauté Garlic and Tomatoes, add Tomato Juice, Basil, Oregano and Brown Sugar; continue to cook 5-10 minutes. Reduce heat to medium if it starts to 'spit'. Pour sauce over the shells and bake 20-25 minutes. While shells are baking, heat the rest of the oil (you should have about 1" in the skillet) and "fry" quickly (approximately 2 minutes) the Turnip, Onion, Beet, and Parsley. Remove with a metal slotted spoon and place on paper towel. Season with Salt and Pepper. Remove shells from oven, sprinkle Vegetable Frites over the shells. Lay a ring of Provolone Cheese on each Pasta Shell and sprinkle the remaining Walnuts over the entire dish. Put Shells back into the oven and bake 5 more minutes.

PASTA SHELLS STUFFED WITH SPINACH RICOTTA,
COTTAGE CHEESE & FRESH TOMATOES

LINGUINE WITH SUNDRIED CRANBERRIES, ROASTED MUSHROOMS & FRESH GRAPES

I find this recipe refreshing, inspiring and delicious with the unusual combinations of simple ingredients. Close your eyes and you will experience savoury, sweet, crunchy, and smooth, which translates into outstanding flavour.

Serves 6

1 1/2 cup Red Onions, cut in 1/4 inch wide strips
1 1/2 cup Red and Yellow Peppers, cut in 1/4 inch wide strips
1/3 cup Shiitake Mushrooms, quartered
1/3 cup dried Cranberries
6 tbsp Galliano Liqueur
3/4 cup Vegetable Stock (can use powered, reconstituted with water)
1/2 cup Kalamata Olives, sliced
5-7 tbsp Grapeseed Oil
2-3 cloves Garlic, minced
1 tsp Basil, dried
1/2 tsp Oregano, dried
24 oz Linguine, cooked, shocked and drained
1 1/2 cup green grapes, sliced lengthwise in half
3 oz Feta Cheese, crumbled
3 oz Pecans
Sea Salt and Cracked Black Pepper

Heat large skillet to med to high heat; add Grapeseed Oil, Onions, Garlic, dried Herbs, Peppers, Mushrooms, and sauté until Onions become translucent. Add Cranberries, Vegetable Stock, Olives and Galliano Liqueur; cook until liquid reduces by half. Add cooked Pasta and Grapes, stir to mix, and continue to cook 5-10 minutes or until all ingredients are hot. Garnish with Feta Cheese and Pecans. Serve on warm plates.

LINGUINE WITH SUNDRIED CRANBERRIES,
ROASTED MUSHROOMS & FRESH GRAPES

DUMPLINGS WITH SEAFOOD BOUILLABAISSE

Hot Dumplings in a delicious seafood broth make this Mediterranean seafood dish a memory in the making as you consume everything down the last drop of liquid!

Serves 6

12 large Shrimp, peeled and deveined
6 Scallops
18 Mussels
3 Garlic Cloves, minced
3-4 tbsp Olive Oil
2 tsp Basil, dried
1 tsp Oregano, dried
6 cups Fish Stock (you may use powdered stock and reconstitute with Water)
3 cups Vegetable Mixture (see recipe on 167)
1 1/2 cup Tomatoes, diced
6 Lemon slices
6 Lime slices
1 cup of White Wine
12 Chive stems
12 Cilantro sprigs
18 Dumplings
Cracked Black Pepper

Dumplings

2 Eggs
2 tsp Basil, dried
1 tsp Oregano, dried
1 tsp Baking Powder
1 tsp Salt
1 tsp Cracked Black Pepper
1 cup Fish Stock, tepid, not hot (you may substitute milk)
1 cup All-Purpose Flour

Make Dumpling Mixture, set aside. The Dumpling Mixture will double in size.

Preheat oven to 400°F

Heat large, ovenproof skillet to medium-high and add Oil, Vegetable Mix, Herbs, Seafood and Garlic. Sauté for 2-3 minutes, add Tomato and cook 2 more minutes. Deglaze with Wine. Add 6 cups of the stock, and Pepper. Drop 1 tablespoon of Dumpling Batter at a time into the broth. Put the skillet into the hot oven for 6-8 minutes or until the Dumplings are cooked and 'puffy'. Carefully remove from oven and put in serving bowls, dividing the dumplings evenly. (Use a slotted spoon to handle Dumplings) Garnish each bowl of bouillabaisse with Lemon, Lime slices, Chive and Cilantro.

In a medium bowl, mix Flour, Baking Powder, Salt, Pepper, dried Herbs and Eggs.
Whisk in tepid Fish Stock until mixture is thick, but not runny.

DUMPLINGS WITH SEAFOOD BOUILLABAISSE

WHOLE WHEAT PASTA
WITH SESAME SEED TIGER SHRIMP & PUMPKIN GLAZE

I combined several flavours from the East with some favourites of the West and came up with a scrumptious tasting and unforgettable pasta dish. I encourage you to step beyond your 'tried and true' pasta recipes and give this a whirl; I know your taste buds will be happy.

Serves 6

1 tbsp Sesame Oil
6 cups Whole Wheat Spaghetti, cooked al denté, shocked and drained
1 cup fresh Pumpkin, peeled, cut into matchsticks (you may substitute butternut squash)
2 tsp Garlic, chopped
2 tbsp Grated Ginger Root (what you do not use can be stored in freezer for later use)
1/2 tsp Red Pepper Chilies
12 oz Large Shrimp, peeled and deveined
2 cups of Bok Choy, finely sliced
4 Green Onions, silvered
Fresh Cracked Black Pepper
2 tbsp Sesame Seeds, toasted

TIPS

A simple way to speed up the prep time with this dish is to cook the pasta the day before making sure you shock it with cold water, thoroughly drain and store it in a zipped plastic bag.

Prepare Hoisin Sauce; set aside.
Cook Noodles until al dente, about 3-4 minutes. Heat skillet on high; add Oil, Garlic, Ginger, Green Onions, Pumpkin matchsticks, Red Pepper Chilies and Shrimp, sauté for 2 minutes. Add Bok Choy and sauté another minute or until just wilted. Stir in the sauce, add pasta and cook until heated through. Taste first and season with a little more Soya, if needed. Add Pepper to taste. Garnish with Sesame Seeds. Serve hot.

Hoisin Sauce

1 cup pureéd Pumpkin; use canned if fresh is not available
4 tbsp Soya Sauce
6 tbsp Liquid Honey
4 tbsp Rice Vinegar
Mix all ingredients together in a bowl until smooth

WHOLE WHEAT PASTA WITH SESAME SEED TIGER SHRIMP
& PUMPKIN GLAZE

rice

These three great staples can easily become the main course, not just a side dish. There are many ways you can add flavour to these staples. I chose these recipes because of their flexibility. For example if you're cooking a dish that calls for lamb and all you have is chicken, then use the chicken. If you're following a recipe that calls for shrimp and you don't have anything you think would work as a good substitute, then omit it completely. Moves like this will not compromise the flavour or strength of your dish, in fact you will begin to develop your own stamp of identity in your cooking. So take a chance and change things up, whether you need to or not.

CHANGE IT UP A LITTLE...

I always suggest using Whole Grain, Basmati, or Jasmine over White Rice, but whatever your choice, it is easy to 'punch up' the flavour of everyday rice. Instead of Water try using things like Chicken, Beef, or Fish Stock — you can even use Fruit Juice like Pineapple or Cranberry. Imagine Pineapple Jasmine Rice served beside your favorite BBQ Chicken. Put a little wow in your rice!

grains and pulses

ARBORIO RICE

This is one of my newest dishes. I particularly like this dish because of the layers and contrasts of flavours. First there are Scallops, seared with the sweetness of Sambuca and Grilled Pears drizzled with Balsamic Vinegar, combined with the smooth texture of Arborio Rice, mixed with ribbons of fresh Spinach, Parmesan Cheese and topped with Parsnip Frites and Walnuts. There must be someone you've wanted to cook a delicious meal for, so try this! I can tell you everyone will experience 'layers of flavour' with each bite, that's for certain.

Serves 6

3 cups uncooked Arborio Rice
6 cups of Vegetable Stock for cooking rice, (may use powder, reconstituted with hot water)
3 tbsp Olive Oil, for cooking rice
3 Parsnips, cut into matchsticks
1/4 cup Oil, for frying Parsnip Frites
18 Scallops
2 tbsp Olive Oil
3 cloves Garlic, minced
3 cups of the following mixed fresh vegetables*
- Red Onion, sliced
- Zucchini, cut into quarters lengthwise and diced
- Green, Red & Yellow Peppers, cored, cut into inch strips and chopped
- Mushrooms cut into quarters
- Turnip, cut into matchsticks 1/2 inch thick
- Eggplant, cut into 1/2 inch slices & diced
- Asparagus stalks, cut diagonally into thirds
2 tsp Basil, dried
1 tsp Oregano, dried
1 cup Vegetable Stock
1 oz White Sambuca Liqueur
2 oz Balsamic Vinegar
1 cup fresh Spinach, washed and cut into ribbons
2 firm Pears, cored and sliced with skin left on
1/4 cup Parmesan Cheese, grated
2 tbsp Butter
6 tbsp Walnuts, chopped

TIPS

Arborio Rice is pronounced "ar-BOH-ree-oh". It takes 17-20 minutes to cook to the al dente stage, which is tender on the outside and firm in the center. It has a beautiful creamy texture and remains tender and moist when cooked. You can use water or stock and even some white wine in your cooking liquid. Arborio likes to be stirred as it cooks.

To cook the Arborio Rice

Heat a large skillet, add 3 tbsp Oil and sauté the rice for a minute or two in order to envelope it with the Olive Oil flavour. Add Vegetable Stock, 1/2 cup at a time, stirring as it cooks and is absorbed. Continue to add stock and cook until the rice reaches the al denté stage. Remove from heat and let the rice sit covered.*

*Cooking the rice can be done a day ahead.

ARBORIO RICE

Make Parsnip Frites

Make Parsnip Frites: Heat 1/4 cup Oil in a sauce pan, drop in parsnip matchsticks and quickly fry to a crisp stage. Place on paper towel and set aside.

Heat a large skillet, add 2 tbsp Oil, Garlic, and Scallops, sauté one minute; add Vegetable Mixture and dried Herbs; sauté for 2 more minutes. Add 1 cup Vegetable Stock, Sambuca, Balsamic Vinegar, Cooked Rice, Spinach and Pear slices. Cook long enough to heat rice through, then turn off heat. Add Parmesan Cheese and Butter, and stir to mix. To serve, evenly divide portions onto 6 plates, allowing 3 Scallops per plate. Sprinkle on Walnuts followed with Parsnip Frites. *You may use any of your favourite fresh vegetable. You want colour, texture and taste.

BARLEY RISOTTO

This is one of my recipes that clearly fits into the 'lifestyle cuisine' kind of cooking. It has layers of flavour all blended together with the Middle Eastern Charmoula. Close your eyes, take a bite and your senses will say…'umm, delicious!'

Serves 6

2 tbsp Butter
1 cup Cooked Black Beans (you can use canned, drain in colander and rinse)
1/2 Garlic Clove, minced
1 tsp Basil
6 tbsp Charmoula (see recipe on page 146)
Cilantro, 4 stems
24 oz. Vegetable Stock (may use quality canned or powder, reconstituted with water)
4 tbsp Parmesan Cheese, grated
Fresh cracked Pepper to taste
2-1/2 cup prepared Pearl Barley*
1 oz Oil
4 oz Sundried Cranberries
1/2 Tomato, diced
6 tbsp Cajun Red Sauce (see recipe on page 138)
6 oz Pecans, chopped
3 cups Mixed Vegetables (Onions, Red and Yellow Peppers, Turnip, Zucchini, Mushrooms, Eggplant and Asparagus or anything you have in the fridge.)

Heat a large frying pan; add Oil, Garlic, Herbs and Vegetables. Sauté on high heat until vegetables are browned. Add Black Beans, Vegetable Stock, Charmoula and Cranberries; reduce heat — allowing mixture to come to a simmer. Add Barley and reduce stock by setting stove on low-medium heat. When the greater part of the stock had reduced, stirring occasionally, then add the butter and reduce again. Stir and add the Parmesan Cheese. Place in a serving bowl, add Cajun Red Sauce and Pecans, garnish with Cilantro.

*Precook the Pearl Barley using the 3 cups of Water to 1 cup of Barley ratio. Bring to a boil, reduce heat and simmer until liquid is absorbed.

BARLEY RISOTTO

BASMATI RICE WITH LAMB

This is one of my signature rice dishes at *3 Guys & A Stove* and is truly an event unto itself! The dish is understated yet classy for an entrée and beyond that, simply great food. 'Basmati' means fragrant...I can smell it already. Start with the aromatic rice, add the delicate flavour of lamb complemented with a wide variety of herbs, spices, vegetables and throw in just enough piquant sweetness from my Red Pepper Jelly and what do you have? *Unforgettable taste!*

Serves 6
12 oz Lamb, cut into pieces
3 cups of Mixed Vegetables (Red & Orange Peppers, Red Onion, Turnip, Zucchini, Asparagus, Mushrooms and Eggplant)
1 1/2 Garlic Cloves, minced
1 tsp Basil, dried
1/2 Oregano, dried
3 oz Raisins
6 oz Black Olives
Pinch of Crushed Chilies (to taste)
3/4 cup Red Pepper Jelly
2 oz. Olive Oil
24 oz Chicken Stock or Vegetable Stock
6 oz Feta Cheese
6 cups Basmati Rice, pre-cooked
Mint leaves to garnish

TIPS

Making it easy: Pre-cooking rice is a great way to cook and perfect rice is easy to get. Simply make sure that you always have two cups of Water for every cup of Rice. I like to put the Rice in before the Water starts to boil, then place the heat on low and cook for 10-15 minutes, or until the rice has absorbed all the Water.

Preheat oven to 400 °F

Heat pan, add oil, braise Lamb for one minute. Add Vegetable Mix, Olives, Garlic and Herbs; stir in pan approximately two minutes. Add Red Pepper Jelly, stir to allowing the jelly to 'breakdown' or 'melt' into the Vegetable Mixture. Add Stock, Chilies, Raisins, and cooked Basmati Rice. Mix well and place into a hot oven cooking until the stock has reduced and absorbed into the rice, about 5-7 minutes. Place in a warmed serving dish; garnish with Feta Cheese and fresh Mint.

*If you are not using homemade Chicken Stock, you can use a stock cube or powder, preferably without MSG, available at the grocery store. Reconstitute with water according to directions on container.

BASMATI RICE WITH LAMB

BEET RISOTTO WITH SWISS CHARD

I prepared this dish with Tiffany Tsuyuki, National Wakeboard Champion. I quite enjoy this vibrant looking and tasty dish. Swiss Chard has great, full-bodied flavour, and the Roasted Beets add sweetness and texture. Sprinkle the Goat Cheese over the top and you have an unstoppable taste.

Serves 6

1 lb. Red Beets, trimmed but not peeled
1 1/2 tbsp Olive Oil
3 tsp Basil, dried
2 tsp Oregano, dried
1 large Onion, chopped
2 Garlic Cloves, finely chopped
1 1/2 cup Sticky Rice precooked
1 1/2 cups Vegetable Stock
2 cups Swiss Chard, wash, dry and shred
Salt and fresh Ground Pepper to taste
1 cup Goat Cheese, crumbled

Tiffany Tsuyuki

Preheat oven to 400°F.

Pierce each beet with a fork. Rub Beets in 1/2 tbsp. of Olive Oil, and dried Herbs, roast in the oven until Beets are tender (about one hour). Cool for 5 minutes and rub off the beet skins. (You may want to use rubber gloves) Dice Beets and set aside. Heat a skillet to medium-high, add 1 tbsp. of Oil, Onion, and Garlic and cook gently to sauté. Add Rice, Stock, Beets, Salt and Pepper, simmer 10 minutes. Garnish with Goat Cheese, shredded Swiss Chard, Salt and Pepper.

BEET RISOTTO WITH SWISS CHARD

CURRIED VEGETABLE RICE
WITH BLUEBERRY YOGURT & MANGO CHUTNEY

Explore the wonderful taste Curry has to offer with this recipe. The sweet heat combination will explode in your mouth and leave you with a tantalizing sensation. Here's cooking at you.

Serves 6

3 cups cooked Rice
12 oz Mixed Vegetables (Onions, Red and Yellow Peppers, Turnips, Zucchini, Mushrooms, Eggplant and Asparagus or anything you have in your refrigerator)
3 oz Raisins
6 tsp Curry
1/2 cup Pineapple
6 tbs Almonds
6 tbs Sweet Coconut, shredded
12 oz Blueberry Yogurt (see tip)
1 3/4 cup Vegetable Stock (preferably without MSG if store bought)
6 tbs Mango Chutney, store bought
6 stem Cilantro, fresh
3 Garlic Cloves, crushed
1 tbs Canola Oil
2 tsp Basil, dried
3 tsp Oregano, dried
12 Shrimp, clean and devein

TIPS

To make your own Blueberry Yogurt, simply combine Yogurt with fresh or frozen Blueberries and stir.

In a non-stick skillet, on high heat add Oil and sauté Shrimp, add Garlic, Vegetables, Pineapple, and herbs. Sauté until vegetables have a little colour, about 1-2 minutes. Add Stock, Curry, Raisins and Rice and reduce heat cooking until liquid has absorbed into the mixture. Stir occasionally if needed. Garnish with Cilantro and serve with the Blueberry Yogurt and Chutney.

CURRIED VEGETABLE RICE WITH BLUEBERRY YOGURT & MANGO CHUTNEY

RICE CRUSTS

This is an excellent healthy and quick alternative to a store bought crust. This crust is very low in fat and can easily be made in advance to lighten the work load.

Serves 6

2 Egg Whites • 1 cup Long Grain White Rice cooked • 1 oz Parmesan Cheese • Cracked Black Pepper and Salt to taste

Cook Long Grain White Rice for 10 minutes in boiling water, and turn it directly into a metal hand sieve or strainer. Put it over 1 inch of boiling Water and cover with a lid. Continue to steam for an extra 5 minutes until it's ready. Turn the rice into a bowl and immediately add the Cheese, Salt and Pepper, and stir very well. Then add the beaten Egg Whites and blend thoroughly. Turn the seasoned Rice-and-Cheese ball into a non-stick pie pan and press it firmly into the pan starting at the center and moving out. Raise the sides about 1/2 inch above the rim. The crust is now ready to be pre-baked before filling. Bake for approximately 20 minutes at 350°F.

CORN AND CRAB PIE WITH CREOLE SAUCE

Serves 6

1 tbsp Olive Oil
1/4 cup Onions, chopped
1/2 cup Green Onions, chopped
1/4 cup Red Peppers, diced
1/4 cup Green Peppers, diced
1 tbsp Garlic, minced
2 cup frozen Corn Kernels
1 pound Crab Meat, lump and drain
2 cups Creole Sauce*
1 1/2 tbsp Cajun Seasoning

Creole Sauce

1 tbsp Olive Oil
1/2 cup Onions, diced
1/2 cup Green Peppers, diced
2 tbsp Garlic, minced
2 cups Tomatoes, peeled and chopped
2 tsp Basil, dried
1 tsp Thyme, dried
2 tsp Cajun Seasoning
Cracked Black Pepper & Salt to taste
2 tsp Worcestershire Sauce
3 cups Fish Stock* (no MSG)
1/2 cups Green Onions, chopped
1/2 cup Celery, diced
1 tsp Oregano, diced

Heat skillet over high heat; add Oil. Add Onions, Celery, Peppers, Garlic and sauté for 1 minute. Stir in Tomatoes, Basil, Oregano, Thyme, Cajun Seasoning, Pepper and Salt to taste. Add Worcestershire and Stock; bring to a boil. Stir in Green Onions and cook over high heat for 12 minutes.

Preheat oven to 375°F

Heat Oil in a large skillet over high heat. Add all the Onions, Green Onions, Red and Green Peppers, Garlic, and Corn; sauté for one minute. Stir in the Cajun Seasoning and cook for one more minute. Gently stir in the Crab Meat and sauté for 2 minutes. Remove from heat. Add Creole Sauce* and mix. Place mixture into Rice Crust*. Bake in oven for approximately 30 minutes. To serve, cut into 6 portions.

RICE CRUSTS/CORN AND CRAB PIE WITH CREOLE SAUCE

Fish Stock

*Fish Stock

3 cups Water

1/4 cup Fish Stock Powder (no m.s.g.)

Bring water to boil, add powder

Reduce heat and simmer, stirring occasionally for

10 to 15 minutes.

SWEET POTATO & SNOW PEA COUSCOUS

The unique blend of ingredients in this dish are absolutely bursting with flavour. The Snow Peas and roasted Sweet Potatoes are a great combination in this easy to make Couscous Dish.

Serves 6

3 cups Couscous
6 cups Vegetable Stock
2 sweet Potatoes, cut into medium sized strips
1 1/2 cups Snow Peas, blanched, shocked and drained
2 tbsp Olive Oil
1/2 tsp Chili Paste (may be purchase in Grocery Store)
1/4 cup Mint, chopped
1/4 cup Lemon Juice
1 tbsp Honey
Salt and Pepper to taste
Mint to garnish

Roast Sweet Potatoes until tender in oven at 400°F
Blanch Snow Peas, set aside. Place Couscous in a bowl and pour boiling Vegetable Stock over the Couscous. Cover and let it sit until the liquid is absorbed. Stir with a fork and add Pepper and Salt to taste. Toss the roasted Sweet Potatoes and Snow Peas into the warm Couscous. Combine Olive Oil, Chili Paste, Mint, Lemon Juice and Honey in small bowl. Pour the dressing over the Couscous and mix. Garnish with mint.

SWEET POTATO & SNOW PEA COUSCOUS SALAD

HERBED HOPPIN' JOHN RICE WITH BLACK-EYED PEAS, BUTTERMILK CORNMEAL CHICKEN

Eating Hoppin' John, a one-pot rice and bean dish is supposed to bring you luck and good fortune. This dish has come a long way from its humble beginning, and is now packed full of delicious colourful vegetables, the tingle of Salsa and tender Cornmeal Chicken, all which produce a wonderful tasting meal. Your destiny is to enjoy this to the fullest!

Serves 6
2 tbsp Canola Oil
6-4 oz Chicken Breasts, boneless
1 cup Cornmeal
3 cups of Rice, cooked and set aside
6 tbsp Tomato Salsa (I like hot, use whatever temperature you like)
1 Onion, sliced
1 Green Pepper, sliced
1 Red Pepper, sliced
1 Yellow Pepper, sliced
1/4 Rutabaga, sliced
1/2 cup Button Mushrooms, sliced
1 cup cooked Black-Eyed Peas (may use canned, please drain)
1 1/2 cups Chicken Stock (may use quality canned or powdered, reconstituted with water)
2 tsp Oregano, dried
2 tsp Basil, dried
2 Cloves Garlic, minced
Cracked black Pepper and Salt to taste
6 flowers fresh Cilantro

Preheat oven to 400°F
Dredge Chicken on both sides in Cornmeal. Heat ovenproof skillet and sauté Chicken in 1 tbsp Oil until golden brown, put in oven to finish cooking. Heat a second pan with remaining 1 tbsp Oil and sauté Vegetables, Black-Eyed Peas, Garlic and Herbs (1 to 2 minutes) . Add Tomatoes, Stock, Salt and cooked Rice. Mix well and put pan in oven until liquid is absorbed. Remove Chicken from oven and slice into strips. Place Chicken on top of Rice, add Salsa and Cilantro to garnish.

HERBED HOPPIN' JOHN RICE WITH BLACK-EYED PEAS,
BUTTERMILK CORNMEAL CHICKEN

REFRIED BLACK BEANS WITH WHOLE WHEAT MEXICAN CORN MEAL TORTILLAS & RED HOT SAUCE

I made these tortillas with actor Grant Nickalls on the television cooking show, *Who's Coming For Dinner*. Grant entertained us with his talent of flipping the tortillas perfectly in the air, which was totally unrehearsed! *Buenos Senior Nickalls!*

Serves 6

Tortillas
1 Egg
1 cup Water
1/2 All-Purpose Flour
1/2 Cornmeal
1/2 tsp each Baking Powder and Salt

Refried Beans
2 tsp Canola oil
1 small Onion, minced
1 Garlic Clove, minced
3 cups cooked Kidney or Black Beans
(may use canned, rinse and drain)
3 drops Hot Pepper Sauce
Salt and Pepper to taste

Red Sauce
28 oz can Tomato Sauce
1 Clove Garlic, minced
1/4 cup Red Sweet Pepper, finely chopped
1 tsp Chili Powder
1 tsp Pickled Jalapeno Pepper
1/4 tsp Ground Cumin
Pinch Granulated Sugar
Fresh Ground Pepper
6 pitted Black or Stuffed Olives, sliced

Additional Ingredients
2 cups Monterey Jack Cheese, shredded
2 cups Lettuce, shredded
1 cup Yogurt, low-fat

Grant Nickalls

In a bowl, whisk Egg and Water. Beat in Flour, Cornmeal, Baking Powder and Salt. Set aside for 10 minutes. Heat a non-stick 7" skillet over medium heat. Brush lightly with vegetable Oil. Stir batter, then pour batter 2 tbs at a time, to make very thin tortilla. Cook just until dry on top, flip once and immediately remove, stacking tortillas until all are cooked. Use paper towels between each tortilla to separate. Stir batter throughout the tortilla making process since cornmeal settles to the bottom.

Heat a non-stick skillet on medium. Add Oil; sauté Onion and Garlic for 5 minutes or until Onion is translucent. Gradually add Beans mashing with the back of the spoon. Cook, stirring often until thickened. Add Hot Pepper Sauce. Season to taste with Salt and Pepper.

In a saucepan, stir together Tomato Sauce, Garlic, Red Pepper, Chili Powder, Jalapeno Pepper, Cumin, Sugar and Pepper and Olives; bring to a boil. Reduce heat and simmer for 5 minutes or until flavours are blended.

Lets Put It Together
Arrange Corn Tortillas into a greased casserole dish. Layer Bean mixture, followed with Red Sauce and Monterey Jack Cheese. Repeat three times. Bake in oven at 350°F for 45 minutes. Remove from oven and add shredded lettuce and yogurt. *OLE!*

REFRIED BLACK BEANS WITH
WHOLE WHEAT MEXICAN CORN MEAL TORTILLAS
& RED HOT SAUCE

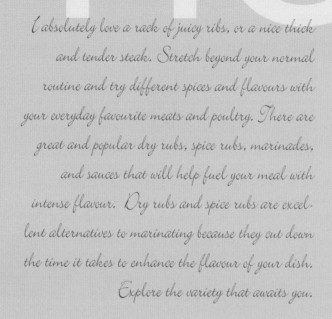

mea

I absolutely love a rack of juicy ribs, or a nice thick and tender steak. Stretch beyond your normal routine and try different spices and flavours with your everyday favourite meats and poultry. There are great and popular dry rubs, spice rubs, marinades, and sauces that will help fuel your meal with intense flavour. Dry rubs and spice rubs are excellent alternatives to marinating because they cut down the time it takes to enhance the flavour of your dish. Explore the variety that awaits you.

SOMETHING TO KEEP IN MIND...

There are really four main things to consider when buying beef from your butcher or grocery store. The type of cut, the marbling of the steak, the trimming of the fat, and most importantly the aging process of the steak. Loin cuts are usually the most tender, and when looking at the marbling look for it throughout the steak. You want to ensure that the fat around the steak is no more than a 1/2 of an inch. When inquiring as to the age of the meat, you should always ask for a steak that has been aged for at least 14 days.

meats

BBQ PORK BACK RIBS WITH GRILLED PINEAPPLE, ROASTED GARLIC & JERK RUB

This is an amazing Jerk recipe and happens to be one of my favourites. The flavour is absolutely intense and has the perfect amount of sweet heat. I love to eat juicy, tender Ribs, I'm sure many of us do, and when they are combined with this delicious Jerk Rub you get a flavour that is out of this world.

Serves 6
6-1 lb Pork Back Ribs
1 fresh Pineapple, cut up into wedges

Jerk Rub
1 Spanish Onion, loosely chopped
3 Cloves Garlic
1 tsp Allspice
1/2 tsp Cayenne
1/2 tsp Cinnamon
1/2 tsp Nutmeg
1/2 tsp Thyme
Salt and fresh cracked Pepper to taste
1 whole Jalapeno Pepper
4 tbsp White Vinegar
1/4 cup Soya Sauce
2 tbsp Sugar

Preheat oven to 350°F
Place Pork Back Ribs in large roasting pan, cover with Water and cover pan with lid or foil and roast at 350°F for 3 hours, pour off Water and allow Ribs to cool. This step can be done the day before and Ribs kept in the refrigerator. Prepare the Jerk Rub by putting all the rub ingredients into a blender and blending until smooth. Put Ribs on BBQ and cook until browned, remove from BBQ and spoon rub over ribs. Turn oven to 450°F and cook 10 minutes. Grill Pineapple wedges on BBQ until grill marks appear. Garnish Ribs with Pineapple. Prepare a "Bird Bath" to wipe fingers clean by dropping a lemon slice into a bowl of warm water; place a fresh cloth napkin with the "bath".

BBQ PORK BACK RIBS WITH GRILLED PINEAPPLE, ROASTED GARLIC & JERK RUB

CHICKEN WITH LEEKS, SWEET POTATOES, APRICOTS, DATES & RAISINS

The dish offers a great unique taste without any hassle in preparation. I love the way the Apricots, Raisins and Dates taste with the Chicken after its time in the oven has allowed extreme flavour saturation. Try and enjoy.

Serves 6

6 boneless, skinless Chicken Breasts, 4 oz each
6 oz Whole Wheat Flour for dusting (may use corn flour)
2 tbsp Olive Oil
2 tsp Garlic, crushed
1 cups Leeks, chopped
2 cups Sweet Potatoes, peeled and cut into chunky sticks, 2 inches long
2 cups of Chicken Stock (powder may be reconstituted with hot water)
1/3 cup Papaya Juice
1/2 tsp cinnamon
1/2 tsp ground Ginger
1/4 cup Dates, chopped
1/4 cup Apricots, chopped
1/4 cup Raisins

Preheat oven to 400°F
Dust Chicken with Flour. Heat a non-stick skillet on medium high, add Oil, brown Chicken on both sides. Place in a baking dish. Using the same skillet, add Olive Oil and sauté Garlic, Leeks, and Sweet Potatoes until softened, approximately 10 minutes, stirring to prevent scorching. Add Chicken Stock, Papaya Juice, Cinnamon and Ginger, Dates, Apricots and Raisins. Simmer 8-10 minutes. Pour Sauce over Chicken; bake 20-30 minutes or until Chicken is cooked.

CHICKEN WITH LEEKS, SWEET POTATOES, APRICOTS, DATES & RAISINS

GRILLED LAMB WITH CREAMY POLENTA, SWEET RED PEPPER & ROOT VEGETABLES

This is one of my favourite Lamb recipes with 'melt in your mouth' taste coming at you from every direction. This is a great dish to impress dinner guests with because each bite will be packed with intense flavour. If you are one of those people who 'don't do lamb', give this a try, the raves you will receive from the recipients who eat it will make you happy you tried it and by then, you'll be hooked on lamb!

Serves 6

1/2 cup each of Carrot, Turnip, Beets, Parsnip, cut into 1" sticks
1/2 cup Onion, sliced
1 1/2 oz Canola Oil
2 Cloves Garlic, minced
1 tsp Basil, dried
1/2 tsp Oregano, dried
8 Sprigs Thyme, fresh
1 cup Chicken Stock (powder may be used, reconstitute with hot water)
24 oz Lamb Loin, trimming excess fat off, cut into 2 oz portions
2 tbsp Dijon Mustard
2 tbsp Mustard Seeds
1 cup Red Pepper Jelly

Polenta

2 cups hot Water • 2 cups Milk
1 cup quick-cook Polenta (cornmeal)
4 oz plain, low-fat Yogurt
Cracked Pepper and Sea Salt

Bring Water, Milk, Salt & Pepper to a boil. Gradually stir in the Polenta a little at a time, stirring constantly so it does not form lumps. Add Yogurt. Polenta may become thick; if this happens just add a little more liquid. Set aside.

Preheat oven to 400°F

Prepare Polenta, set aside. Place Onion, Carrots, Turnips, Beets, Parsnip, Oil, Garlic and Thyme, in oven-safe dish and roast in oven for 30 minute. Heat oven-safe large skillet on high heat, add Oil, and sear to brown Lamb on both sides. Remove from heat and spread Dijon mustard over the Lamb. Roast in oven until desired level of cooking is reached; 10 minutes will give you medium rare, which is what I recommend. While Lamb is in oven, prepare the Sauce. In a separate pan, melt Red Pepper Jelly over medium heat; add Chicken Stock and Mustard Seeds, reducing mixture to a syrup texture, stirring constantly. Remove roasted Vegetables from oven and add half the Red Pepper Jelly to vegetables, stirring to mix. Remove Lamb from oven and allow it to stand for 10 minutes so that juices will seal.

To assemble: Divide Polenta into six portions and place onto a serving platter, spoon vegetable mixture over each Polenta portion, followed with two medallions of Lamb per Polenta, drizzle remainder of sauce over all six portions, add Salt and Pepper to taste. Garnish each portion with fresh Mint.

GRILLED LAMB WITH CREAMY POLENTA, SWEET RED PEPPER & ROOT VEGETABLES

INDIAN RUB ROASTED CHICKEN BREAST WITH COCONUT RICE & CARAMELIZED BANANA

Want to give Roasted Chicken a delicious taste dimension? Try this easy rub that offers a robust blend of Moroccan spices combined with the mild taste of Coconut Rice and the delicious flavour of Caramelized Bananas. Captivate your senses while you savour each bite!

Serves 6

Rub
1 tsp ground Coriander
1 tsp ground Ginger
1 tsp ground Turmeric
1 tsp ground Cumin
1 tsp ground Paprika
1 tsp Salt
1/2 tsp ground Cardamom
1/2 tsp Cayenne Pepper
2 Garlic Cloves, minced
2 tbsp Olive Oil
6 Chicken Breasts, skinless, about 4 oz

Coconut Rice
2 cups Long or Short Grain Rice
3 cups cold Water
1 Cinnamon stick
1 cup Coconut Milk, low-fat
4 tsp Sugar

Caramelized Banana
3 firm Bananas, peeled and halved lengthwise
1/3 cup Sugar
1 tsp ground Cinnamon

Combine all Spices and Oil in a small bowl, and rub on Chicken before grilling or pan-frying

Place the Rice in a colander and wash well. Place the Rice, Water, Coconut Milk and Cinnamon stick in a saucepan over medium to high heat and bring to the boil. Cover tightly and reduce the heat to low and cook for 10 minutes or until the water has been absorbed. Add the Sugar, over the saucepan and place over very low heat for an additional 5 minutes.

Sprinkle Bananas with Sugar and Cinnamon. Preheat a non-stick skillet over high heat and spray lightly with Oil. Cook the Bananas for 2 minutes on each side or until the Sugar has caramelized. To serve this tasty dish place the Coconut Rice on your serving plates and top with the Banana slices. Place the grilled Chicken beside the Rice and enjoy.

INDIAN RUB ROASTED CHICKEN BREAST WITH COCONUT RICE
& CARAMELIZED BANANA

PAN SEARED VEAL WITH ASIAN CRAB & YOGURT HOLLANDAISE

This very simple yet quite elegant dish is a delicious mouth-watering experience. This is not your standard Hollandaise sauce, it is my Yogurt Hollandaise and tastes like no other you have had, plus it is quick and easy to prepare. The veal peaks in flavour with the addition of the Cajun spice and crab cakes add great texture. The whole package will melt in your mouth when you drizzle the Yogurt Hollandaise on the top...truly an amazing dish. Do not deny yourself the pleasure of eating this dish!

Serves 6
12 oz Veal Tenderloin, cut into 1 oz medallions (2oz per portion)
Cajun Spice (enough to dredge medallions into blacken)
1/2 tbsp Olive Oil
6 oz Asian Crab (1oz per serving)
1/4 cup rolled Oats
2 Egg Whites (save yolks for hollandaise below)
1/8 cup Parsley, chopped
1/2 tbsp Dijon Mustard
1/4 medium Onion, diced fine
Salt and fresh ground Pepper to taste

Yogurt Hollandaise
3 Egg Yolks
1 cup low-fat Yogurt
3 tbsp White Vinegar
1/2 tsp Cayenne
Juice of 1 Lemon
Salt and Pepper to taste

TIPS

What's the difference between my Yogurt Hollandaise and traditional Hollandaise? Both taste great, but mine is significantly lower in fat by using Yogurt in place of Butter without sacrificing any flavour.

Pre heat oven to 425°F
Pound each Veal Medallion and dredge in Cajun Spice. Heat skillet to medium-high; add oil and quickly brown both sides of Medallions. Remove the Medallions from heat. In a large bowl, combine Asian Crab, rolled Oats, Egg Whites, Parsley, Dijon Mustard, Onion, Salt and Pepper. Form into 6 cakes. Place Asian Crab cakes on Veal Medallions; pour Hollandaise over the Crab and Veal. Bake in oven for 5-10 minutes or until Crab is hot throughout. Serve immediately on warmed plates.

Bring water to a boil in a double boiler. In the top boiler pan, vigorously whisk the Egg Yolks and Yogurt, until the mixture becomes thick and creamy. Take off the heat and whisk in Vinegar, Cayenne, Lemon Juice, Salt and Pepper. Set aside.

PAN SEARED VEAL WITH ASIAN CRAB & YOGURT HOLLANDAISE

STUFFED TURKEY WITH HORSERADISH, SUNDRIED CRANBERRY & SWEET PEPPER RELISH

I prepared this with comedy dynamo Johnny Gardhouse who acted like a judge when I asked him to pound out the Turkey Breast. He took the meat mallet and used it as a gavel, yelling to the live audience..."*Order in the court, I say Order!*" His antics brought the house down with laughter, but the finished product produced nothing but praise. Who can argue with comedy and success all at the same time?

I love the taste this recipe offers, not to mention the colorful presentation, which is a precursor to the excellent flavour you will experience. Every bite is accompanied with an amazing taste sensation. Once you try this, I'm pretty sure you will see that Turkey can be easy and is for any time of the year.

Serves 6
2-12 oz Turkey Breasts, boneless
8 oz Ricotta Cheese, partly skimmed
1 cup Spinach, chopped
1 tsp Basil
1/2 tsp Oregano
1 tbsp Olive Oil
Salt and Pepper to taste
1 cup fresh Cranberries

Relish
7 oz jar of Hot Horseradish
8 oz can Cranberry Sauce
1 oz Sundried Cranberries
1/4 Red Pepper, finely chopped
1/4 Yellow Pepper, finely chopped

Johnny Gardhouse

Preheat oven to 375°F

Using a meat mallet, pound the Turkey Breast until it is approximately 1/2" thick. in a bowl, combine Ricotta Cheese, Spinach, Salt and Pepper; stir to mix. Divide mixture evenly between two Turkey Breasts. Roll up Turkey Breast, sprinkle with Herb mixture and rub on Oil. Wrap in foil and roast in oven for 1 hour and 15 minutes. While Turkey is in oven, make Relish by combining all Relish ingredients in bowl; stir and set aside. When cooked, remove Turkey from oven and let stand for 10 to 15 minutes. Slice and place on a warm serving platter. Finish dish by spooning relish over Turkey strips, garnish by sprinkling fresh Cranberries over entire dish.

STUFFED TURKEY WITH HORSERADISH, SUNDRIED CRANBERRY &
SWEET PEPPER RELISH

CHICKEN WITH THAI RED CURRY & COCONUT MILK

Thai food is a favourite of mine because it offers harmony and balance of taste, aroma, texture and flavour, in other words; I think it is delicious. If you have not ventured into Thai flavoured food, you need to try this. A well-stocked grocery store has most of the ingredients you need to prepare Thai dishes. The Red Curry blended with Coconut Milk marries beautifully with the Pineapple and Chicken to create an unimaginable level of taste. This is easy and fast to prepare, so how about trying your hand at Thai cooking.

Serves 6

1 tbsp Canola Oil
4 tsp Red Curry Paste (medium)
6 boneless skinless Chicken Breasts
1 Onion, sliced
2 Sweet Red Peppers, cut into thin strips
1 cup Pineapple, cubed
1 Lemon, grated rind
1 cup light Coconut Milk*
4 tbsp Fish Sauce (Found in most grocery stores. For a lighter taste, look for light coloured sauce)
1 fresh Lemon, squeezed
1/2 cup fresh Cilantro, chopped

TIPS

Look for Light Coconut Milk at your grocery store. Powdered is sometimes available if canned cannot be located. Common Thai ingredients are Lime, Lemon, Fish Sauce, (which acts as Thai Salt substitute), Coconut Milk, Chili Peppers, Red Curry and Cilantro.

Preheat oven to 400°F

Heat skillet to medium-high, add Oil and pan-sear Chicken Breast to a golden brown on both sides. (You are only browning, not cooking through). Transfer Chicken to a baking dish and roast in oven approximately 10 minutes. In the same pan as the Chicken was pan-seared; sauté Onion, Red Pepper and Pineapple until Onion becomes transparent. Add Curry Paste, Coconut, Fish Sauce, and Lemon rind and reduce heat to simmer. While mixture is simmering, remove Chicken from oven and cut into thin strips, add Chicken strips to mixture and continue to simmer for 3-5 minutes. Serve over your favourite Rice.

CHICKEN WITH THAI RED CURRY & COCONUT MILK

LEFTOVER PORK WITH BOK CHOY, SHIITAKE MUSHROOM & THAI SAUCE

Please do not let any ingredients scare you off and keep you from preparing this easy Thai dish. Check out my notes on bok choy below. Even though I used leftover Pork Tenderloin, you can use any cut of Pork or leftover Chicken.

Serves 6

1/3 cup of Soy Sauce
3/4 cup Sugar
2 small Red Chilies, seeded and chopped
1 1/2 tbsp shredded fresh Ginger
3 tbsp Fish Sauce
3 tbsp Lime Juice
1 head Bok Choy cut into 4" length pieces.
8 oz Shiitake Mushrooms, cut into quarters
1 1/2 lbs precooked (leftover portions) Pork Loin or Pork Tenderloin
1 tsp Sea Salt (to be used in boiling water)

Bok Choy is like getting two vegetables in one; the white stalks are sweet and tender, even to eat raw and the leaves are like Swiss Chard or Spinach. If you cannot use Bok Choy, you may substitute Napa Cabbage, Kohlrabi, Broccoli stalks, Savoy Cabbage, Celery, or Fennel bulb.

Place the Soy Sauce, Sugar, Chillies, Ginger, Fish Sauce and Lime Juice in a pre-heated non-stick skillet, and cook over medium heat, stirring for 4-5 minutes or until the mixture thickens slightly. Slice the Pork and add to the liquid. Cook for 4 minutes or until hot. In a separate pan, add Water, Sea Salt and bring to a simmer. Add Bok Choy and Mushrooms to the simmering Water until the Bok Choy wilts and becomes tender, but not mushy. Remove from Water and drain. Place the steamed Bok Choy and mushrooms onto a serving platter. Arrange Pork pieces on top of Bok Choy and drizzle the sauce over Pork and Vegetables. Serve right away.

Cooked Rice Noodles are great with this dish.

LEFTOVER PORK WITH BOK CHOY, SHIITAKE MUSHROOM & THAI SAUCE

LAMB CASSEROLE
WITH CURRIED SWEET FRUITS & PINK LENTILS

This recipe offers a bit of the flavour, taste and aroma of Morocco. The scents of Onion, Curry, Garlic, and Lamb mingle with the sweetness of Pineapple, Coconut, Raisins and Mint, making this dish robust with flavour.

Serves 6
3 tbsp Garlic Puree
2 pinches Basil
1 pinch Oregano
12 oz Lamb Leg Roast, diced
1/2 Turnip, cut into matchsticks
1 Red Onion, chopped
3 oz Mushrooms, quartered
1 each, Green, Red and Yellow Peppers, chopped
2 Zucchini, chopped
1 cup Pink Lentils, par cooked according to directions on package
36 oz Chicken Velouté*
6 tbsp Curry Paste or Powder
1 tbsp Olive Oil
1/2 cup Raisins
1/2 cup Pineapple, diced
1 oz Almonds, sliced
1 1/2 oz Sweet Coconut, shredded
Fresh Mint to garnish

*Chicken Velouté
1 cup Chicken Stock Powder
4 cups Water
1 cup Flour

Preheat oven to 425°F
Heat a large ovenproof skillet on medium-high, add Oil, Garlic, Lamb and Herbs; sauté until Meat is golden brown. Add Vegetables and sauté for 2 minutes. Add Velouté, Lentils, Curry, Pineapple and Raisins and cook for 3 minutes. Pour into casserole dish; sprinkle with Coconut and Almonds. Cover and put into hot oven and bake for approximately 40 minutes. Remove cover and bake for an additional 10 minutes. Garnish with fresh Mint.

Bring Water to boil, add Powder, reduce to simmer, mix Flour with one cup of Water and mix, put through strainer and add to Chicken stock. Whisk constantly, simmer 10 minutes.

LAMB CASSEROLE WITH CURRIED SWEET FRUITS AND PINK LENTILS

CHARBROILED BEEF TENDERLOIN

When you are a meat lover, nothing beats the thrill of a beautiful steak, cooked to perfection and seasoned just right with the traditional favourite, peppercorn sauce. This is easy to make and turns a steak into a mouth-watering experience.

Serves 2

2 – 7oz Beef Tenderloin (Ask your butcher for centre cut)
2 tbsp Peppercorns, cracked (use a rolling pin)
1 tbsp Olive Oil
2 Garlic Cloves, minced
2 oz Red Wine
1 pkg of Powdered Demi-glaze, preferably without MSG or **you can make your own from beef bones and marrow

TIPS

Aged meat is preferred for better flavour and tenderness. Get to know your butcher in your grocery store or butcher shop, their expertise is valuable. Demi-glaze is 1 part beef stock with 1 part brown sauce, sometimes with Madeira, cooking until it reduces by half leaving you with a rich and beautifully flavoured base for various sauces. It is a labour intensive job but offers satisfying results. Let me know if you make it.

Make Demi-glaze according to instructions on package, set aside.

Preheat oven to 425°F. Heat an ovenproof skillet to medium-high; add Oil and pan sear Steak on both sides, (you are searing to brown sides only). Temporarily transfer Steaks to a plate. Put Garlic and cracked Peppercorns into skillet and sauté 1 minute, deglaze skillet with Red Wine, reducing liquid by half. Add Demi-glaze and heat through. Put Steaks back in skillet, spooning sauce over the top and put in hot oven until desired level of doneness.

CHARBROILED BEEF TENDERLOIN

GRILLED STRIPLOIN WITH ROASTED HORSERADISH & SEARED ROSEMARY RED ONION

Incredible, tender and juicy, this king of Steaks is a sizzling success with the zippy Horseradish, Garlic, seared Onions and grilled Rosemary.

Serves 2

2 – 12 oz Striploin, 1/2 inch trimmed
2 Garlic Cloves, minced
3 tbsp Olive Oil
1/4 Red Onion, cut into rings
2 large fresh Rosemary Sprigs
4 tbsp Creamy Horseradish

TIPS

Turn a steak over just once during the cooking time. Always use tongs, not a fork. If you want to salt your steak, do so after you have cooked it, salt interferes with the searing process.

Preheat oven to 425°F
Mix together the Horseradish, Garlic and 2 tbsp Oil; set aside. Heat an ovenproof skillet to high, add 1 tbsp Oil; pan-sear both sides of steaks (you are searing to brown sides only). Remove Steaks from skillet and put in Onion and Rosemary, lay Steaks back in skillet on top of Onion mixture. Spoon Horseradish mixture over the top of Steaks and put into hot oven until desired level of doneness. Serve on warmed plates laying seared Onion and Rosemary over Steaks.

GRILLED STRIPLOIN WITH ROASTED HORSERADISH
& SEARED ROSEMARY RED ONION

CHICKEN CASSEROLE WITH POLENTA, MARJORAM SCENTED GOUDA & FRESH GRAPES

Nothing brings people together like sharing a yummy, piping hot casserole. This easy to make savoury casserole captures and blends the taste of creamy Polenta, roasted Vegetables, moist Chicken, mellow and rich Gouda Cheese crust and fresh Grapes, creating an unforgettable taste!

Serves 4

4 - 4oz Boneless Chicken Breasts browned in a skillet. When cooked, remove & cut into strips. Set aside.
6 oz Gouda Cheese, divided into 4 equal parts
2 cups of Chicken Velouté*
2 cups total of the following vegetable combination: (or use your favourite vegetables)
- Turnip cut into matchsticks
- Onion, chopped
- Asparagus stalks, cut into 1-inch pieces

8 tbsp Cornmeal
1 cup of Green Grapes, divide 'clusters' into 4 equal sections
1 tsp Basil, dried
1/2 tsp Oregano, dried
Sea Salt & cracked fresh Pepper to taste
2 tbsp Olive Oil
1 tbsp Garlic, minced

*Chicken Velouté
1 cup Chicken Stock Powder
4 cups Water
1 cup Flour

Preheat oven to 425°F
Heat large skillet to med-high; add Oil, Garlic and sauté Vegetable Mixture until Onion is transparent, add Basil, Oregano, Salt and Pepper. Add cooked Chicken strips. Pour in Chicken Velouté and stir over medium heat and add cormeal until mixture thickens slightly. Spray Casserole dish with Oil and spoon in mixture. Cover dish and bake for 20 minutes. Remove cover and place Gouda Cheese on top, continue to bake 10 more minutes. Remove from oven and garnish with Grape clusters.

Bring Water to boil, add Powder, reduce to simmer, mix Flour with one cup of Water and mix, put through strainer and add to Chicken stock. Whisk constantly, simmer 10 minutes.

CHICKEN CASSEROLE WITH POLENTA, MARJORAM
SCENTED GOUDA & FRESH GRAPES

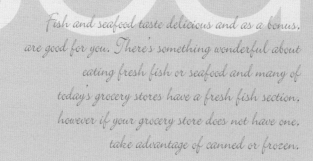

Fish and seafood taste delicious and as a bonus, are good for you. There's something wonderful about eating fresh fish or seafood and many of today's grocery stores have a fresh fish section, however if your grocery store does not have one, take advantage of canned or frozen.

My favourite way to prepare fish is by first pan-searing and then finishing it in the oven. The oven time allows the fish to soak up the flavours of the ingredients used in the recipe. I finished all these recipes in the oven and believe you will like the results so much, you'll be 'hooked' on this method.

JUST GIVE IT A LITTLE TOUCH...

It's very easy to cook a fish fillet without over or under cooking it. Fish responds well to a light touch. If your indentation jumps back then its done, however if the indentation stays its undercooked and needs a bit more oven time. If the light touch causes the fillet to separate then its overcooked.

od

seafood

BLACKENED PACIFIC TUNA WITH GOAT CHEESE, SHIITAKE MUSHROOM & FRESH LAVENDER

This show-stopping, upscale Tuna dish is stupendous in taste and presentation! The combination of blackened Tuna and Goat Cheese is superb giving you extraordinary taste. It is so popular at *3 Guys & A Stove* we actually sell out of it some evenings. The dish is easier to put together if you prepare the Brown Rice and Garlic puree ahead. It is important to have a skillet or two; you can heat to a very hot temperature. Once you have made this, you will be so proud.

Serves 6

6 Tuna fillets (7oz each)
4 tbsp Canola Oil
6 tbsp Goat Cheese
12 Shiitake Mushrooms, sliced
1 tsp Basil
1/2 tsp Oregano
2 Cloves Garlic, crushed
1 tsp Salt
3 cups cooked Fish Rice (receipe below)
12 slices of Lime
12 Lavender Sprigs, fresh
6 Cilantro Flowers

Fish Rice

2 Cloves Garlic, crushed
1 tbsp Canola Oil
1 tsp Basil
1/2 tsp Oregano
12 oz Cooked Black-Eyed Peas (drain and rinse if using canned)
1 cup Tomatoes, diced
1 cups Fish Stock*
3 cups of cooked, Whole Grain Brown Rice
2 1/2 cups assorted Vegetables, chopped

Preheat broiler on oven. Heat a non-stick skillet; add 1/4 tbsp Oil, sear Tuna quickly on one side just to darken (approx. 1 minute) turn over and sear second side (approx. 2 minutes). Tuna will be undercooked at this point. Spread 1 tbsp Goat Cheese over top of each fillet. Mix Garlic, remaining Oil and Herbs, and drizzle over each fillet. Place Shiitake Mushrooms on each fillet and put 2 Lavender Sprigs into Cheese on each fillet. Broil in oven 2-3 minutes (this is for medium rare, broil longer if you prefer medium - be careful not to overcook). Place Fish Rice on 6 plates and a Fillet on each plate, garnish w/Lime slices and Cilantro.

Preheat oven to 425°F
Heat a non-stick skillet, add 1 tbsp Oil, and sauté Vegetables, Black-Eyed Peas, Garlic and Herbs, 2-3 minutes. Add Tomatoes, Stock and Rice. Mix and put in oven at 425°F for 7-9 minutes or until hot

BLACKENED PACIFIC TUNA WITH GOAT CHEESE
SHIITAKE MUSHROOM & FRESH LAVENDER

CRAB CAKES WITH BANANA CURRY & CRANBERRY YOGURT

The enormous amount of flavour packed into these little cakes is amazing. Your taste buds will cry for more.

Serves 6
12 oz Crabmeat
2 tbsp Oatmeal
1 Egg White
1 tbsp Dijon Mustard
1/8 cup Parsley, freshly chopped
2 tbsp Tandoori Spice
1/2 cup Whole-Wheat Flour
3 tbsp Olive Oil
3 tbsp Sundried Cranberries
1/4 cup Yogurt
2 tbsp Cranberry Juice
1/4 cup Pineapple Juice
1 Banana
1 tbsp Yellow Curry Powder
Cilantro Sprigs to garnish

Mix Crabmeat, Oatmeal, Egg White, Dijon Mustard and Parsley, together in a bowl. Shape into cakes about 1-1/2 inch in diameter by 3/4 inches high. Mix Tandoori and Flour together in another bowl. Dust each Crab Cake into mixture on both sides. Heat non-stick skillet, add Oil and cook on both sides until Crabmeat is cooked. In two separate bowls, stir 3 tbsp Cranberries, Yogurt and Cranberry juice, set aside. In second bowl, mix Pineapple Juice, mashed Banana and Yellow Curry Powder. Place Crab Cakes on a platter, drizzle Cranberry Yogurt over half of each Crab Cake and Pineapple-Banana mixture over the other half. Garnish with Cilantro Sprigs.

CRAB CAKES WITH BANANA CURRY & CRANBERRY YOGURT

GROUPER WITH DATES, APRICOT & SWEET CRANBERRY PINEAPPLE RELISH

Grouper is a firm-textured, yet mild and delicate flavoured fish and when matched with the Cranberry Pineapple Relish, you open the door for extreme multi-layered flavouring.

Serves 6

3/4 cup of a Honey-nut type of cereal, crushed
1 1/2 lbs Grouper, cut into 6 serving-sized pieces
2 Egg White, lightly beaten
1 tbsp Butter, soft
2 tbsp Canola Oil
Sea Salt and Pepper

Cranberry Pineapple Relish

2 tbsp Demerara Sugar
1 1/2 cups Orange Juice
1/4 cup Dates, chopped
1/4 cup Apricots, chopped and dried
1/4 cup Pineapple, chopped
1/4 cup whole Cranberries
2 tbsp Butter
2 tbsp Cornstarch
4 tbsp Pineapple Juice, cold (or any sweet fruit juice)

Preheat oven to 425°F

In food processor, process Cereal until fine, and place in shallow dish. Dip Fillets into Egg Whites and then into Crumb Mixture to coat both sides. Heat an ovenproof skillet to medium-high; add Oil and Butter; brown both sides of Fish, season with Salt and Pepper and put skillet in oven for 10-12 minutes to finish cooking or until Fish flakes easily when tested with fork. Warm 6 dinner plates. Serve Cranberry Pineapple Relish over each piece of Grouper. Serve Grouper with your favourite Rice.

To prepare the Relish, heat a saucepan to medium; add ingredients and bring to a simmer. Mix the Cornstarch with cold Pineapple Juice and add to the simmering fruit, cook until mixture thickens. Remove from heat to cool.

GROUPER WITH DATES, APRICOT AND SWEET CRANBERRY PINEAPPLE RELISH

HALIBUT WITH CHERRY TOMATO SAUCE & BLACK OLIVES

This is a great way to cook Halibut. By giving all the ingredients time to unlock their total potential, you can create a powerful taste sensation. The flavour from the Cherry Tomatoes and Black Olives is outstanding. If you are not too big on Halibut, do not be afraid to replace it with Sole, Flounder or Turbot, all are equally tasty and will go just as well with the recipe.

Serves 6

1 1/2 lbs Halibut, cut into 6 serving-sized pieces
2 tbsp Olive Oil
1 tsp Garlic, crushed
1 1/2 cups Mushrooms, sliced
1 cup Onions, chopped
1 tsp Chili peppers
3 cups Cherry Tomatoes, halved
3 tsp Basil, fresh
3 tsp Oregano, fresh
2 tsp Demerara sugar
1/2 cup of sliced Black Olives
2 tbsp fresh Parmesan Cheese, grated

Preheat oven to 425°F

Spray baking dish with Vegetable Oil. In a large non-stick skillet, add Oil; sauté Garlic, Mushrooms and Onions until softened, approximately 3 minutes then add the Chili Peppers. Add the Tomatoes, Basil, Oregano, Sugar and Olives and simmer for another 3 minutes. Place Halibut in baking dish large enough to arrange in a single layer; pour Tomato mixture over top. Bake 10-15 minutes or until fish flakes easily when tested with fork. Serve sprinkled with fresh Parmesan Cheese.

HALIBUT WITH CHERRY TOMATO SAUCE & BLACK OLIVES

SEARED SALMON WITH MUSTARD SEEDS, HONEY, ROASTED ALMONDS & COCONUT MILK

Ordinary to extraordinary! This dish combines some of the best flavours of the land. You will taste the sweetness of Honey and Coconut, the texture of Almonds and Mustard Seeds, the flavor of Salmon and Spinach, heightened with Garlic and Chillies. Do yourself a 'flavour' and make this dish.

Serves 6

6-4oz Fillet Salmon
1 tsp Chili Peppers
1 can Coconut Milk - light
1 oz Almond slivers, roasted*
1/2 Lemon, squeezed
2 Garlic Cloves, minced
1 oz Canola Oil
6 cups Spinach leaves, washed and dried
6 Lime slices

Honey Rub
1/4 cup Honey
3 tsp Mustard Seeds
3 Sprigs fresh Mint, chopped

Preheat oven to 300°F
*Roast Almonds by putting them in small pan, place on oven until golden. Remove from oven and reserve for later use. Place Mustard Seeds on one side of wax paper, fold paper in half, and 'crack' Seeds by running a rolling pin back and forth. Rub each Salmon Fillet with Honey Rub. Heat skillet on med-high, add Oil, sauté Salmon until golden, turn over, and sauté second side. Transfer Salmon to baking dish and put into oven at 300°F. Use Salmon skillet, add Garlic, Lemon Juice, Chilies and Coconut Milk, and heat thoroughly. Drop in Spinach to just wilt & remove immediately. Arrange Spinach mixture into six portions. Place a Salmon Fillet on each Spinach mixture; ladle Coconut Milk over each fillet. Garnish with Lime slice.

To make Honey Rub, mix together Honey, Mustard Seeds and Mint.

SEARED SALMON WITH MUSTARD SEEDS, HONEY, ROASTED ALMONDS AND COCONUT MILK

MUSSELS

I enjoy Mussels enormously and slurp up every drop of the liquid in the bowl. I have watched people sop up the juice with the rolls we leave at the table when this dish is ordered. If by chance you have never tried preparing Mussels, I encourage you to give this a go…it is truly a very easy dish and I am betting that once you have prepared and eaten these, you will be adding them to your list of *'recipe hits'*!

Serves 2
1 lb Mussels
6 oz Fish Stock*
2 tbsp Garlic Puree (olive oil combined with minced fresh garlic creating a 'runny paste')
1/4 cup Carrot, cut into matchsticks
1/4 cup Turnip, cut into matchsticks
1/4 tsp Basil, dried
1/8 tsp Oregano, dried
Green Onions stalks to garnish
6 Lemon Slices

Simply place all ingredients in a large skillet, cover, and steam on med-high heat approximately 4 minutes or until the Mussels open. Once they have finished, place them in a big pasta type bowl and garnish with the Green Onion stalks and Lemon Slices.

*You can use store bought powdered Fish Stock and reconstitute it with water. I like to look for labels with no MSG.

MUSSELS

TROUT SPICED GREEN ROLLS WITH SHIITAKE MUSHROOMS AND CRISPY RICE NOODLES

These tasty rolls are an adventure in the making and eating. The multi-dimensional flavouring will make each bite a unique moment to remember. If you have another favourite fish you would rather use, go ahead and use it. Let's get rolling!

Serves 6

12 leaves Bok Choy, separate leaves and wash, quickly blanch and set aside
2 Limes (the juice of one and 12 slices of the other)
12 oz Trout, skinned & boned, cut into 1/2" pieces
1/2 cup Shiitake Mushrooms, diced
1/2 cup Green Peas, uncooked
1/2 cup Water Chestnuts, sliced
1 tsp fresh Grated Ginger
1/2 cup Onion, diced
1/2 cup Carrots, diced
3 oz Hoisin sauce (President's Choice product)
1 1/2 cup Rice Noodles (vacuum packed in grocers) lightly crunch
1/2 cup Canola Oil (for frying)

Sauce

2 cups Hoisin Sauce
1/4 cup Soya Sauce
1/4 cup Cemerara Sugar
1/4 cup Rice Vinegar
3 tsp roasted Sesame Seeds
1 tsp red Chilies

Preheat oven 350°F

Prepare stuffing by mixing Mushrooms, Peas, Water Chestnuts, Ginger, Onions, carrots, 3 oz Hoisin Sauce, and Trout pieces. Set aside. Prepare sauce simply by mixing all ingredients together and set aside. To assemble rolls: Place 2 tbsp of Stuffing Mixture on bottom part of blanched Bok Choy Leaf, start to roll up towards darker top of Leaf. When you get to the top, tuck sides of Leaf under and place seam side down in a sprayed baking dish. Pour the sauce Mixture over top of rolls. Bake 30 minutes at 350°F. While Rolls are baking, heat a Wok on medium-high heat, add Oil, heat Oil and quick fry Noodles. Ladle them out as soon as they crisp. Remove Rolls from oven; Garnish with 12 slices of Lime and Crunchy Noodles.

TROUT SPICED GREEN ROLLS WITH SHIITAKE MUSHROOMS
& CRISPY RICE NOODLES

SWORDFISH WITH GRILLED TOFU, BLACK BEAN SAUCE AND MANGO CHUTNEY

Swordfish has a mild flavour with firm, meaty flesh and offers a delicious taste sensation. The grilled Tofu, Black Bean Sauce and Mango come together to perform an amazing dance for your taste buds to enjoy. If you are not big on the Tofu simply omit it and move on.

Serves 6
6 x 5oz portions of Swordfish
6 oz Black Bean Sauce (store bought)
3 oz Mango Chutney (President's Choice product)
6 tbsp Tofu, diced
12-oz Fish Stock (can use powder, reconstitute with hot water)
1/2 each Red, Yellow and Green Pepper, sliced
2 Garlic Cloves, minced
3 Bananas
Fresh Mint for garnish

TIPS

If you cannot find fresh swordfish, substitute: Grouper, Halibut, Mahi-Mahi, Rockfish, Red Snapper or Tuna.

Preheat oven at 350°F
Roast Peppers with Garlic for 30 minutes; let cool and slice. Reduce oven heat to 300°F. Grill Swordfish, 3 minutes on first side, 3 minutes on second side. In a saucepan, add Fish Stock, Black Bean Sauce, Tofu and Peppers, heat thoroughly. Remove Fish from grill and place the Sworfish on serving dish, drizzle with Sauce, add Chutney and garnish with Banana and Mint.

SWORDFISH WITH GRILLED TOFU, BLACK BEAN SAUCE AND MANGO CHUTNEY

BLACK TIGER SHRIMP
WITH COCONUT & CHILI VINEGAR

I have seen people squabble over who gets to eat the last Coconut Shrimp! These shrimps, dipped in the Chili vinegar will melt in your mouth. They are addictive so be prepared to eat more than one...

Serves 6
36 large Black Tiger Shrimp, peeled and deveined
3 cups Coconut
1/2 cup Flour
4 Eggs, beaten
4 cups Oil for frying
36 Lime slices
Cilantro, washed and dried to garnish

*Chili Vinegar
6 oz Rice Vinegar
1 tbsp Crushed Chilies

Mix and set aside.

TIPS

If the oil is not hot enough, the shrimp will absorb it and become heavy, but if it is too hot, the outside will burn and the inside will remain uncooked. Fry no more than 6 shrimp at a time so that they will not stick together and you can stay on top of this process. Oil should be at 350°F

Prepare the Chili Vinegar* set aside. Devein the Shrimp by making a slit along the back or outside of the Shrimp, lifting out the black vein, discard the vein. Rinse the Shrimp. In three separate shallow bowls, put Flour in bowl one, Eggs in bowl two and Coconut in bowl three. Dip Shrimp first in the Flour, then Eggs followed with Coconut, laying them on a baking sheet as you complete this process with all the Shrimp. In a deep saucepan, heat oil to 350°F degrees.

Deep-fry Shrimp, placing them on several layers of paper towel until all the Shrimp is finished. Serve immediately with Lime Slices and Cilantro and dip Shrimp into Chili Vinegar.

BLACK TIGER SHRIMP WITH COCONUT & CHILI VINEGAR

BLACKED STUFFED TIGER SHRIMP
WITH CAJUN RED SAUCE

This dish can be addictive and I will wager, 'you can't eat just one,' I know I can't. This is a fun dish to make where everyone in the kitchen prepares a step in the recipe, all while anticipating the delicious dinner that waits.

Serves 6
24 large [21-25 count] Shrimp, peeled, devein and butterfly*
1 cup Asian Blue Crab, drained
1 Egg White
1 tbsp Dijon Mustard
1/4 cup fresh Parsley, chopped
24 slices of Peameal Bacon, pounded thin with a mallet
3 tbsp Cajun Spice
3 tbsp Canola Oil

Cajun Red Sauce
3 oz can of Tomato paste
1 tbsp of Cayenne Pepper
1-8 oz can of Tomato Juice
1 oz of Worchester Sauce
1 tsp Basil, dried
1/2 tsp Oregano, dried
2 tsp Liquid Honey
To make Cajun Red Sauce heat a saucepan on medium; add all ingredients and simmer for 20 minutes.

TIPS

How to butterfly Shrimp: Peel the shrimp, discarding shells. Leave the tail on. Cut the Shrimp 3/4 open lengthwise, being careful not to cut in half. Lay the Shrimp flat on a cutting board follow the outside curve of the Shrimp with a paring knife, cutting halfway into the body of the Shrimp. Open up the Shrimp, rinse under cool running water and remove the black vein. Lay Shrimp on paper towels.

As the Cajun Red Sauce is simmering on low, prepare the Shrimp. *(See tip above).* Preheat oven to 400°F. In a separate bowl, put Crab, Dijon Mustard, Parsley, Egg White and mix. Place into the Shrimp, leaving the shrimp tail facing up. Wrap all the Peameal Bacon around the Shrimps, the tail will be sticking out. Roll the wrapped Shrimp in the Cajun Spice. Heat a large heavy, ovenproof skillet on medium-high, add oil and 'Blacken' all sides of the Shrimp, approximately 2-3 minutes. Put the skillet in the hot oven for 10 minutes. Remove and put 1/2 tsp of Cajun Red Sauce on each Shrimp. Serve.

As you can see, I serve this over Creamed Pasta, but you can serve it with Rice, Pasta, or even a Baked Potato.

BLACKED STUFFED TIGER SHRIMP WITH CAJUN RED SAUCE

GRILLED SCALLOP & MARINATED ARTICHOKE SALAD

You have a fantastic tasting salad when you take creamy, sweet tender Scallops, roast them with the mild flavour of Artichokes, spice them up a bit with Citrus, Garlic and Seasonings and place them on a soft, colourful bed of Mixed Greens.

Serves 6

9 cups of Mixed Greens
18 Scallops
10-12 canned Artichokes, drained and cut in half
1 tsp Basil, dried
1/2 tsp Oregano, dried
3 Cloves Garlic, minced
3 tbsp Olive Oil
6 oz Rice Vinegar
1 Lemon, sliced into rings
1 Lime, sliced into rings
12 Chive Stems

TIPS

What does it mean to Deglaze? It is a way to add a lot of flavour to your recipe. Deglazing liquid can be Wine, Stock, Water or almost any liquid, in this recipe I use Rice Vinegar. The liquid loosens up anything that has stuck to the pan, producing a better tasting liquid that truly enhances the dish.

Preheat oven to 425ºF

Heat a large skillet on medium-high, add Oil, Garlic, Scallops, Artichokes and Herbs; immediately put skillet in the hot oven and roast the mixture approximately 4-7 minutes. Remove the pan from the oven and deglaze (See tip above) with the Rice Vinegar. Put equal portions of Greens on 6 plates, pour Artichoke and Scallop mixture over the Greens. Garnish with Lemon and Lime slices and Chive Stems.

GRILLED SCALLOP & MARINATED ARTICHOKE SALAD

With vegetables it's quite simple: the fresher they are, the richer the taste. A farmers' market is a great place to buy local produce, very fresh and usually very clean. There might be seasons when it's easier to buy frozen vegetables, like peas and corn. You can add them to a dish to increase taste and colour. New and different vegetables are widely available at grocery stores and I encourage you to pick some up and give them a try. I believe by incorporating new vegetables into your cooking, you will not only eat better, but also enjoy new heights of flavour, taste, and texture.

That's totally exciting!

JUST IN CASE...

If there is a vegetarian in the family, and you wish to avoid cooking two separate meals, try to use recipes where the Meats, Poultry, Seafood, etc. can be cooked separately and added once the meal is served. For example a Rice dish that calls for Lamb or Shrimp can easily be made with one of the servings being vegetarian. Try and see how this method can simplify the cooking process.

ables

vegetables

BALSAMIC ROASTED TOMATOES & RED ONIONS

This simple and quick side item offers a great accompanying flavour to any meal. If you want to give this dish more 'umph', try adding your favourite Cheese to top this tasty treat off. Get out there and explore.

Serves 6

12 ripe Cherry Tomatoes, halved
2 red Onions, thinly sliced
3 tbsp Olive Oil
4 tbsp Balsamic Vinegar
4 tbsp Granulated Sugar
4 tbsp Oregano Leaves, fresh or 2 tbsp dried

Preheat the oven to 400°F
Place the Cherry Tomatoes, in an ovenproof dish. Sprinkle Red Onions around Tomatoes. Combine the Oil, Balsamic Vinegar, Sugar, Oregano and pour over the Tomatoes and Onion. Bake for 20 minutes, making sure the Tomatoes are soft.

BALSAMIC ROASTED TOMATOES & RED ONIONS

CHARMOULA

This is a great way to add loads of leveled flavour to your favourite soup, fish, pasta, and meat. And leftovers are great, simply freeze the rest in ice cube trays, once frozen, pop out of the tray and store in a freezer bag in the freezer. When you want to use Charmoula you just grab a cube and get cooking.

Serves 6
6 tbsp Garlic
2 tsp Cumin
2 tsp Paprika
1 tsp Sea Salt
1/2 tsp Cayenne
1/2 tsp Cracked Fresh Pepper
1 cup Parsley, chopped
1/ 2 cup Cilantro, chopped
6 tbsp fresh Lemon Juice
4 tbsp Olive Oil

Blend all ingredients in food processor.
Yields: 2/3 cup use 1 tbsp per portion serving in each recipe.

CHARMOULA

RED-SKINNED POTATO
WITH MUSTARD SEED DRESSING

This tasty simple Vegetable dish blends with any of your BBQ favourites and goes great beside a delicious lunchtime sandwich. Basic ingredients like the Mustard Seed, Cider Vinegar and fresh Rosemary make this vegetable dish come alive and pop with flavour.

Serves 6

2 lb Red Skinned Potatoes, cooked and cut into cubes
1 tsp Mustard Seeds
1/8 cup Cider Vinegar
1/2 cup low-fat Yogurt
1/4 cup Parsley, chopped
1 tsp Cracked Black Pepper
2 Sprigs Fresh Rosemary, snipped with scissors into little pieces

Whisk the Mustard Seeds, Cider Vinegar, low-fat Yogurt, Parsley and Black Pepper together until smooth with a wire whisk. Pour the dressing over the Potatoes using a soft spatula to coat the Potatoes without crumbling them. Garnish with fresh Rosemary.

RED-SKINNED POTATO WITH MUSTARD SEED DRESSING

POTATOES BAKED IN CIDER VINEGAR & SEA SALT

This is a very simple way to turn everyday Baked Potatoes into a mouth-watering experience. All you really need are Baking Potatoes, Vinegar, and Salt to be on your way to a delicious side dish.

Serves 6
6 small (4 oz each) Baking Potatoes, washed and dried
1 cup Cider Vinegar
1/3 cup Coarse Sea Salt
Foil Wrap

TIPS

Leftover Potatoes can can be used to create Gourmet Pizza. By putting leftovers into the microwave and taking the chill out of them, you can stir in some Egg Whites, season with Basil, Oregano and Salt, then mix in enough Flour so that the dough stops sticking to your hands, spread your dough onto a pan, add your pizza sauce and favourite toppings, and you've got yourself a gourmet sensation. Imagine a Potato crust pizza with fresh spicy Sausage, Red Onions, and Provolone Cheese. Now that's what I'm talking about; explore the possibilities.

Preheat oven to 425°F
Put Vinegar in a deep bowl, pierce each Potato with a fork. Dip Potatoes in Cider Vinegar. Sprinkle each Potato with Sea Salt. Wrap each Potato in foil; bake 30 minutes in the oven. Tear foil exposing top-half of Potato and continue to bake 10 more minutes to crisp up the skin. Remove from oven, completely unwrap and serve.

POTATOES BAKED IN CIDER VINEGAR & SEA SALT

SPICED TOFU WITH STEAMED GREENS

This is a great recipe for the Tofu lovers out there. The spiced Tofu, fresh Ginger and steamed Spinach will leave your mouth watering. For those that don't care for the heat but still love the Tofu, try using regular Tofu and omit the Red Chilies.

Serves 6
24 oz sliced firm Tofu (1/2 inch thick)
5 tbsp Hoisin Sauce
1 cup Rice Vinegar
3 tbsp grated fresh Ginger, grated
1 tsp of Small Red Chillies, Seeded and chopped
1 cup Chicken Stock, powder and canned are available at your grocer (no MSG)
6 cups of Whole Leaf Green Spinach, washed and dried

Vegetable Stock
3 tsp Vegetable Stock powder
1 cup Water
Mix together, bring to boil and simmer 5 minutes

TIPS

Tofu is like a sponge for flavour, so don't be afraid to use spices and ingredients that impart lots of taste like the fresh Ginger and Chillies above. Firm Tofu from the refrigerator section is usually a better quality and keeps its shape while cooking. When you want the tofu to 'disappear' as in a dessert, use soft, which crumbles easily.

In a frying pan, place Hoisin Sauce* (receipt on page 70), Rice Vinegar, Ginger, Chilies and Vegetable Stock. Cook on medium heat for 4 minutes. Add sliced firm Tofu and simmer for 3 minutes or until heated through. Place Spinach on top of Tofu, cover, and heat quickly. Place Spinach on plate, place Tofu over Spinach, and pour the Sauce over the Tofu.

SPICED TOFU WITH STEAMED GREENS

WILTED SPINACH & ONIONS WITH CIDER

This easy and full-flavoured dish is best to serve the moment the Spinach is wilted, so have everything ready to go, making it the last 'to-do' item before the meal.

Serves 6

12 cups baby Spinach, washed, drained cutting off any unsightly ends
1 large Onion, chopped
2 tsp Olive Oil
1/4 cup Cider Vinegar
1/4 cup Sugar
Salt and fresh Ground Pepper

Heat skillet to medium-high, add Oil and sauté Onion to just a light brown colour. Pour in Cider Vinegar and Sugar, heat until Sugar dissolves. Place Spinach in the Cider mixture and continually stir to accommodate for the 12 cups. Remove Spinach and drain in Colander the moment it wilts. Place on Platter and serve immediately.

WILTED SPINACH & ONIONS WITH CIDER

YORKSHIRE VEGETABLES

I prepared this tasty and 'easier than you might think' dish with actor Derek McGrath on the television cooking show, *Who's Coming For Dinner*. Derek got right into this and helped me produce a delicious slant on an old favourite. Try it and 'wow' your family and friends!

Serves 6
1 small Eggplant, trimmed, halved and thickly sliced
1 Egg
1 cup All-purpose Flour
1 1/4 cups Milk
2 tbsp Thyme Leaves, fresh
1 red Onion, cut into quarters
2 large Zucchini, slice
1 Red and 1 Yellow Bell Pepper, cut into wide strips
4 tbsp Canola Oil
2 tbsp Parmesan Cheese, grated
Salt and Pepper to taste
3 Sprigs each of Fresh Rosemary and Marjoram to garnish

Derek McGrath

Beat the Egg in a bowl, gradually beat in the Flour and a little Milk to make a smooth thick paste. Slowly pour in the rest of the Milk, add the Thyme Leaves and Seasoning to taste and stir until smooth. Leave the Batter in a cool place until required.

Preheat over to 425°F
Put the Oil in a shallow baking pan and heat in the oven. Add the prepared Vegetables, toss them in the Oil to coat thoroughly and return the pan to the oven for 20 minutes. Give the Batter another whisk, then pour it over the Vegetables and return to the oven for about 30 minutes or until the Batter is puffed up and golden. Reduce the heat to 375°F for about 10 minutes, or until edges are crisp. Sprinkle with Parmesan Cheese, Rosemary and Marjoram.

YORKSHIRE VEGETABLES

ROASTED ROOT VEGETABLES

These Vegetables release such a wonderful flavour! As you can see by reading the recipe, the only time this recipe takes is in the cutting up of the Vegetables, so hand a friend a knife and chop and talk; you will be done in quick fashion and the taste is scrumptious.

Serves 6

1/2 cup each of Carrot, Turnip, Beets, Parsnip, cut into strips
1 cup Red Onion, chopped
4 cups Button Mushrooms, quartered
1/2 Red Pepper, chopped
1/4 Yellow Pepper, chopped
1/4 Green Pepper, chopped
1 Zucchini, chopped
1/2 cup Eggplant, cut into 1/2 inch slices and diced
1/2 cup Asparagus, cut into 1 1/2 inch pieces
1 1/2 oz Olive Oil
3 Cloves Garlic, minced
1 tsp Basil, dried
1/2 tsp Oregano, dried
8 Sprigs fresh Thyme
Sea Salt and Cracked Pepper

TIPS

Save any leftovers, if there are any and use them in soups, casseroles, frittatas, and salads.

Preheat oven to 450°F
Mix the Oil and Garlic together, pour over the Vegetables, tossing to coat Vegetable Mixture, season with Basil, Oregano, Thyme, Salt and Pepper. Put in oven and roast for 12 minutes or until slightly browned and tender.

ROASTED ROOT VEGETABLES

VEGETABLE CASSEROLE WITH WHITE BEANS, PESTO & COUSCOUS

This Casserole has all the makings of good old comfort food with a continental twist and flavour. If you are lucky enough to have any leftovers, you will enjoy them just as much, if not more, the second day, but that's only if you are lucky!

Serves 6
6 cups of Vegetable Mixture* (recipe on page 161)
3 Garlic Cloves, minced
2 tbsp Olive Oil
1 1/2 cup pre-cooked White Beans, drained (Navy, Great Northern or your favourite)
4 tbsp Charmoula (See page 146)
6 cups of Vegetable Volouté**
1 1/2 cups Tomato, diced
2 tsp Basil, dried
1 tsp Oregano, dried
12 tbsp Couscous

**Vegetable Velouté
1 cup Vegetable Stock Powder • 4 cups Water • 1 cup Flour

Bring Water to a boil, add Powder, reduce to simmer, mix Flour with one cup of Water and mix, put through strainer and add to Vegetable Stock. Whisk constantly and simmer for 10 minutes.

Prepare Velouté; keep warm. Preheat oven to 400°F Heat skillet to medium-high; add Oil, Vegetable Mixture, Garlic, and Herbs and sauté until Onion becomes transparent. Add Charmoula and cook 4 more minutes. Stir in Velouté, White Beans, Tomatoes and Couscous, mix thoroughly and pour into a sprayed casserole dish, cover and bake for 20 minutes. Remove cover and continue baking 15 more minutes. Serve.

*Roasted Vegetable Mixture
Potato, diced and par-cooked Red Onion, sliced thinly
Zucchini, cut into quarters lengthwise and diced
Green, Red and Yellow Peppers cored, chopped and cut into 1/4 inch strips
Mushrooms cut into quarters
Turnip, julienne 1/2 inch thick
Eggplant, cut into 1/2 inch slices and diced

VEGETABLE CASSEROLE WITH WHITE BEANS, PESTO & COUSCOUS

ROASTED PUMPKIN STIR FRY WITH SALTED CASHEWS & GRAPEFRUIT

Pumpkin is more than pies; it is a super food that is super delicious, especially prepared this way. The Grapefruit gives an exciting kick of flavour, while the Cashews offer a wonderful crunch, and the sauce is pure goodness, making this dish an experience to savour.

Serves 6

3 cups of fresh Pumpkin, cut into matchsticks (substitute Butternut Squash if Pumpkin is not available)
2 Grapefruit, peeled and sectioned
1 cup Salted Cashews
1-2 tbsp Canola Oil
1 red Onion, cut into rings
1 tsp Basil, dried
1/2 tsp Oregano, dried
1 sweet red pepper, cut into matchsticks

Hoisin Sauce

1/2 cup puréed Pumpkin; use canned if fresh is not available
2 tbsp Soya Sauce
3 tbsp Liquid Honey
2 tbsp Rice Vinegar
Mix all ingredients together in a bowl; set aside.

TIPS

Substitute Pistachios for Cashews since they are from the same family. Hoisin Sauce is a great sauce on Ribs, Chicken or anything you like to BBQ. Serve with your favourite Rice, Pasta or even a Baked Potato.

Make Hoisin Sauce; set aside.
Heat a large skillet on high; add Oil, Onions, Pumpkin, Grapefruit, dried Herbs, and Sweet Red Pepper and sauté until Onions become transparent. Add the prepared Hoisin Sauce and cook until Pumpkin is tender, 6-10 minutes. Serve over a bed of your favourite Rice.

ROASTED PUMPKIN STIR FRY WITH SALTED CASHEWS & GRAPEFRUIT

GRILLED BUTTERNUT SQUASH
WITH GRATED NUTMEG & OKA CHEESE

The natural sweetness of the Squash, Maple Syrup and Raisins combined with the crunch of Cashews and the smooth nutty flavour of the Oka Cheese makes this vegetable dish outstanding.

Serves 4
1 Butternut Squash, about 1 pound
1 tbsp Butter, melted combined with 1 tbsp Oil
1 tsp Basil, dried
1/2 tsp Oregano, dried
1 1/2 cups Oka Cheese, flaked (use a carrot peeler)
4 tbsp Cashews, lightly toasted
1/4 cup Raisins
Fresh Cracked Black Pepper
Sea Salt
1 tsp Nutmeg, freshly grated
2 oz Maple Syrup

Preheat oven to 400°F
Cut the Butternut Squash in half lengthwise and scoop out the seeds with a spoon. Mix together Butter/Oil combination and brush the cut surfaces with the mixture. Sprinkle with Sea Salt, Cracked Pepper, Basil and Oregano. Put the Squash in a baking dish and place in heated oven for 1 hour or until cooked. Remove from oven. When the Squash is cool enough to touch, scoop out the flesh, being careful not to tear the skin. Dice the flesh and put it into a bowl and add 1 cup of the flaked Oka Cheese, Nutmeg, Raisins, and Maple Syrup; toss well. Spoon the mixture back into the shells. Garnish with the Oka and Cashews and place under the broiler until golden brown.

GRILLED BUTTERNUT SQUASH WITH GRATED NUTMEG & OKA CHEESE

ROASTED VEGETABLE FRITTATA
WITH HOT TOMATO SALSA

You know what I love about Frittatas, they are versatile; from young to old, anyone can make them, using just about any of your favourite foods. Roasted Potatoes and Vegetables are high on my list of favourite foods, with Shrimp and Salsa not far behind, so pull out the skillet and make a Frittata tonight!

Serves 2
6 Eggs
4 oz Vegetable Mixture, roasted*
6 large Shrimp, peeled and deveined**
2 oz Oil
1 tsp Basil, dried
1/2 tsp Oregano, dried
3 tbsp Black Olives, sliced
4 oz Salsa
4 Chive Stems
4 Cilantro Stems
Cracked Pepper
4 tbsp Parmesan Cheese, grated

TIPS

Eggs taste better when served warm and an easy way to keep them warm is to heat your plates in the toaster oven on 200°F. Use hot pads when handling the plates!

Preheat oven to 450°F
Pour Oil over the vegetables, tossing to coat Vegetable Mixture, season with Basil and Oregano. Put in oven and roast for 12 minutes or until slightly browned and tender. Cool slightly. Save any leftover Vegetable Mixture and use in soups, casseroles, and salads.
In a bowl, mix Eggs, Vegetable Mixture, Olives and Herbs. Heat a large skillet on medium high, add Oil and sauté Shrimps for 2 minutes, turn down heat to low and add the Egg mixture. Cook until almost set which allows you to 'flip over'*, the Egg Mixture. Turn off heat allowing the Frittata to finish with only the heat of the pan. Serve on warmed dinner plates with 3 scoops of Salsa on each plate. Garnish each plate with Cilantro and Chives. If you are not comfortable flipping the Frittata - simply pop it in the oven to finish cooking.

**Devein the Shrimp by making a slit along the back or outside of the Shrimp, lift out the black vein, discard the vein. Rinse the Shrimp.

*Roasted Vegetable Mixture
Potato, diced and par-cooked
Red Onion, sliced thinly
Zucchini, cut into quarters lengthwise and diced
Green, Red and Yellow Peppers cored, chopped and cut into 1/4 inch strips
Mushrooms cut into quarters
Turnip, julienne 1/2 inch thick
Eggplant, cut into 1/2 inch slices and diced

ROASTED VEGETABLE FRITTATA WITH HOT TOMATO SALSA

Many people I talk to say that they don't have the time or energy to make their own fresh homemade desserts, instead they use prepackaged, store bought desserts that usually contain high quantities of sugar and fat. Others tell me they don't make desserts because of the difficulty or complexity of many recipes. I decided to offer you some of my tastiest dessert recipes that are made quickly. Most of my desserts are simple and hassle-free so you can be comfortable and relaxed as you prepare them. Of course everything will be exploding with flavour and isn't that what you want with a dessert?

DON'T BE AFRAID TO EXPERIMENT...

Don't waste time with elaborate recipes. Quick, easy, and full of flavour is the best way to go. Remember cooking can be a great way to relax and have fun. The more you try the better you become.

desserts

BLACK BING CHERRIES WITH VANILLA BEAN FROZEN YOGURT

The multi-leveled flavouring in this dish is truly magical. Each bite of these extra sweet juicy Cherries is bursting with the perfect amount of flavour intensity. The taste heightens as the Cherries cook with Cranberry and Orange Juice, seasoned with Cinnamon…need I say more?

Serves 6
18 oz Bing Cherries with juice
6 Cinnamon Sticks
1/4 cup Orange Juice
1/4 cup Cranberry Juice
1/4 cup Honey
1/4 cup Sugar
18 oz Vanilla Frozen Yogurt
6 Sprigs Mint
3 tablespoons Cornstarch
3 tablespoons cold Water

First, pour the liquid from the can of Cherries into a saucepan, retaining the Cherries for later. Add Orange Juice, Cranberry Juice and Cinnamon sticks and bring to a boil. Add 3 tablespoons Sugar. Remove Cinnamon sticks from sauce and retain for dipping into Honey and Sugar. Mix the Cornstarch with equal amounts of Water and blend, add to Sauce and cook until thickened. Reduce to simmer and add Cherries. Place Honey in a bowl; pat remaining Sugar in a separate bowl. Dip Cinnamon sticks into Honey and then roll into Sugar. Scoop Frozen Yogurt into individual serving dishes, cover with Cherries and drizzle the Sauce. Garnish with Honey, Cinnamon, Sugar stick and Sprig of Mint.

BLACK BING CHERRIES WITH VANILLA BEAN FROZEN YOGURT

CANTALOUPE ALASKA WITH FROZEN VANILLA YOGURT & MINT MERINGUE

Yogurt is a great food to use with fruits. The next few recipes are simple ways to have fresh and elegant desserts without fuss.

Serves 6

1/2 liter Frozen Vanilla Yogurt
1 Ripe Cantaloupe
4 Large Egg Whites, at room temperature
1/4 tsp Cream of Tartar
1/4 cup Sweetener

TIPS

Save those Egg Yolks, they can be used to thicken sauces, custards, salad dressings or added to a quiche. Mixed with a bit of water, Egg Yolks can be used as a glaze over the top of breads and pastries. Always keep refrigerated.

Scoop Vanilla Yogurt into 6 balls, each large enough to fit into cavity of a wedge of Melon. Place scoops on baking sheet covered with parchment and put in freezer until solid. When ready to serve, preheat oven to 500°F. Cut a Cantaloupe into 6 wedges, scoop out all seeds. Cut a small slice off the outside bottom so the wedges sit flat. Beat Egg Whites in large bowl with electric mixer on low speed until foamy. Add Cream of Tartar and beat on high speed until soft peaks form. Beat in sweetener and continue to beat until whites form stiff peaks, glossy, and shiny.

Place Cantaloupe wedges on an ovenproof dish. Fill each wedge with a frozen scoop of Yogurt. Spread Meringue over the top of the Frozen Yogurt and Melon, leaving rind uncovered. Make peaks in the Meringue with the back of a spoon. Bake in hot oven for 3-5 minutes or until golden brown. Garnish with fresh Mint and serve immediately.

CANTALOUPE ALASKA WITH FROZEN VANILLA YOGURT
& MINT MERINGUE

CHOCOLATE STRAWBERRY CAKE
WITH ROASTED BANANA AND COCONUT

The name says it all here. I love the combination of Chocolate and Strawberries, and when mixed with the Roasted Banana and Coconut Sauce you will be asking yourself how you ever lived without it. They will line up to try this.

Serves 8

16 large Strawberries (2 cups), smashed
8 Eggs, Whites only
1 cup Demerara Sugar
1/2 cup Unsweetened Dutch-Processed Cocoa Powder
1 cup Grape-Nuts™ cereal
Light Vegetable Oil Cooking Spray
4 Strawberries to garnish
3 tsp coconut, toasted for garnish

Roasted Banana and Coconut Sauce
3 Bananas, unpeeled
1 1/2 tsp freshly squeezed Lemon Juice
1 tsp Rum Flavoring
6 oz light Coconut Milk

Preheat oven to 350°F. Place unpeeled bananas in the oven, roast until they soften, and turn dark, about 15 minutes. Carefully remove Bananas from the oven and while they are cooling, begin cake. Combine the smashed Strawberries, two of the Egg Whites, Sugar, and Cocoa Powder in a large mixing bowl. Stir to mix well. Add the Grape-Nuts™ cereal and mix with a wooden spoon. Set aside. Using an electric mixer beat the remaining Egg Whites at medium speed until they form stiff, dry peaks. Add a third of the beaten Egg Whites to the Strawberry-Cocoa mixture and stir to combine. Add remaining Egg Whites, and fold gently until completely incorporated.

Spray the bottom and sides of a 9-inch spring-form pan with Vegetable Oil. Pour the batter into the pan, gently shake, or tap to even the top and get rid of any air bubbles. Bake for about 25 minutes, until the Cake is firm to the touch in the center and the sides begin to pull away from the pan. Remove from oven, place the pan on a rack, and cool. The Cake will shrink a bit as it cools.Remove Cake from spring-form and place on serving dish. Pour the sauce over the Cake and serve. Garnish with Coconut and fresh Strawberries

Heat a saucepan; add Coconut Milk, heat to warm while Coconut Milk is warming, peel the Bananas, mash with a fork and add to the Coconut Milk. Cook 3-4 minutes. Remove from heat. Add Lemon Juice and Rum Flavoring and stir mixture.

CHOCOLATE STRAWBERRY CAKE WITH
ROASTED BANANA & COCONUT

STRAWBERRY ALMOND BLUEBERRY PIE

Easy as pie sums it up here! This dessert utilizes only six ingredients and is fabulous. Serve it at your next dinner party or as a great treat for you family. From start to finish, it is done in under an hour, so let's get baking

Serves 8

1 1/4 cups Rolled Oats
1 / 4 pure Maple Syrup
2 cups strawberries, quartered
2 cups Blueberries
2 1/3 cups Demerara Sugar
1/2 cup Dry Roasted Almonds, chopped

TIPS

Try using your favorite fruits as an alternative. Blackberries, Raspberries, and Peaches are great with this recipe. Explore the possibilities.

Preheat oven to 375°F.

In mixing bowl, stir 1/4 cup of almonds, 1 cup Rolled Oats, Maple Syrup, and 3 tsp of Demerara Sugar. Pour into deep-dish pie pan and press to mold the sides and bottom. Bake at 375°F for 10 minutes. Remove from oven and turn oven temperature up to 425°F. In a mixing bowl, put Strawberries, Blueberries, and 2 cups Sugar; mix. Put into a pie crust. Combine the remaining Almonds, Oats and Demerara Sugar and sprinkle over the pie. Return to oven and bake for 30 minutes. Remove and place on cooling rack.

STRAWBERRY ALMOND BLUEBERRY PIE

KEY LIME YOGURT FREEZE WITH FRESH KIWI

Sweet and tart, yet smooth and creamy, there is nothing like the clean flavour of Lemon and Lime to wake up your taste buds. I have combined island citrus with creamy Yogurt, added color and more flavour with Kiwi to create a scrumptiously light dessert. Your brain says… 'No fat, incredibly low calories', your mouth just says, 'Wow'.

Serves 8
1 fresh Lemon, squeezed for juice
1 fresh Lime, squeezed for juice
3 cups Low-fat Yogurt
2 tsp Artificial Sweetener
1 Kiwi Sliced
2 Mint Leaves

In food processor or blender, mix Yogurt, Lime and Lemon Juice and Sweetener. Then pour into desired containers (you can use goblets, dessert fruit cups, crystal bowls). Put into freezer for 2 hours. Garnish with Kiwi and Lime slices in each dish.

KEY LIME YOGURT FREEZE WITH FRESH KIWI

SUGAR CRUSTED APPLE PEAR TART

I wanted a warm, fresh fruit, not too sweet tart with different textures to bite into, so I roasted some Almonds, grated some Cinnamon, sprinkled dried Cranberries & drizzled Maple Syrup over the top. Just one more ingredient; frozen Vanilla Bean Yogurt. *Oh yeah, I definitely got what I wanted!*

Pastry

Makes enough for 24 tart shells and lids,
(Only use half of the pastry -
Freeze the other half for later use)
1 lb Vegetable Shortening
5 cups All-purpose Flour
1/4 tsp Salt

Tart Filling

6 Apples, cored and sliced
6 Pears, cored and sliced
1/2 silvered Almonds, gently roasted either on top of stove or in oven
1 tsp Cinnamon
1/2 cup dried Cranberries

Topping

1/4 cup dried Cranberries (reserve for garnish)
1 oz per tart of Pure Maple Syrup
1 scoop per tart of Frozen Vanilla Bean Yogurt

TIPS

When you make pastry, keep all the materials as cold as possible. Ice water helps the pastry stay tender. Try to give the pastry time to rest and chill for at least an hour before rolling it out. Over-handling can cause pastry to be tough. Producing fine pastry is a pleasure and rewards you with great taste.

Mix together with pastry blender until you get pea-size lumps. In a 1 cup measure, whisk with a fork; 1 Egg and 2 tsp White Vinegar. Add enough cold water to fill the 1 cup measure. Add Egg mixture to Flour Mixture, mixing with a fork until dough is moist. Shape dough into a ball, chill at least 1 hour. Divide in half, roll out Pastry Dough with a rolling pin to 1/8" thick. Cut into 4" rounds and press into cupcake pans. Cut out 12 lids and keep chilled until ready to place on filled tarts.

Preheat oven to 400°F
Mix ingredients together, fill the tart shells, and cover with a pastry lid and bake 15 – 20 minutes or until golden brown. Remove from oven. Place on a cooling rack.
Carefully remove from tins.

To serve, place tart on plate, place 1 scoop of Frozen Yogurt on top, drizzle 1 oz of Maple Syrup over Tart and Frozen Yogurt and sprinkle a couple of reserved Dried Cranberries to garnish.

SUGAR CRUSTED APPLE PEAR TART

BAKED APPLES WITH COCONUT & VANILLA BEAN

Smell the delicious aroma of Baked Apples, fragrant Sweet Coconut flesh and subtle hints of Vanilla. The scent is intoxicating as it wafts through your kitchen.

Serves 6

6 Apples
1/2 cup Shredded Coconut
1 tsp All-purpose Flour
2 oz low-fat Vanilla Yogurt
3 tsp Demerara Sugar
6 pieces of Vanilla Bean (See tip below)
6 tsp Honey

TIPS

Vanilla beans are long and thin like skinny black string beans. They are available at many grocery stores and/or bulk food stores. Vanilla Beans flavour many different foods. You can use them whole or cut them open and let the seeds out. Imagine heating maple syrup with a whole vanilla bean and pouring it over fresh strawberry pancakes.

Preheat oven to 350°F

Core Apples, scooping out some of the flesh and score around the middle of the skin. Make a filling of the Coconut, Flour, Yogurt and Demerara Sugar. Spoon into the Apples and top with a piece of Vanilla Bean. Bake in oven for 40 minutes or until soft. When Apples are baked - remove from oven and glaze with Honey

BAKED APPLES WITH COCONUT & VANILLA BEAN

WHITE CHOCOLATE CHEESECAKE

This is the first time I have ever shared this recipe. Many of you have asked, but I was not ready to share it until now… it is my signature dessert and it is divine. Making this is labour intensive, but the results are beyond any Cheesecake you have ever tasted. This is my 'pièce de résistance' in desserts; I share it proudly with you.

Serves 8

Crust

1 3/4 cup Graham Cracker crumbs (that's about 16 crackers)
6 tsp Unsalted Butter, melted
1 tsp Sugar

Butter a 9x3-inch springform pan. Combine Graham Cracker Crumbs, Butter and Sugar in a food processor, (use the metal blade). Process until well blended. Press evenly over bottom and two thirds up sides of springform pan.

Filling

10 oz White Chocolate, broken up
1/2 cup Whipping Cream, (35% cream), at room temperature
2 packages (8 oz each) Cream Cheese, at room temperature
4 large Eggs, separated and at room temperature
4 tsp Vanilla
Dash Salt

Preheat oven to 300°F. Melt White Chocolate in top of double boiler over simmering water. Slowly stir in Cream, stirring until smooth. Remove from heat and cool slightly. Beat Cream Cheese in large bowl with an electric mixer on medium speed until smooth. Add Egg Yolks one at a time, blending well after each addition, stopping to scrape down sides of bowl and beaters once or twice. Add White Chocolate, Vanilla and Salt. Beat at medium speed for 2 minutes. Beat Egg Whites in a separate mixing bowl on low speed until foamy. Beat on high speed until soft, rounded peaks form. Fold Whites into chocolate mixture. Pour into crust.

Place pan on baking sheet and bake in oven for 55 minutes. The cake will rise and the top will jiggle slightly when shaken. Turn off oven and let the cake stay in the oven for 1 hour. Gently run a rounded knife around the side of the pan. Be prepared for the cake to sink. Remove to a wire rack and completely cool to room temperature. Cut into 14 equal pieces. *See tips on cutting.

Topping

1 box Phyllo Pastry, thawed (found in the freezer section of your grocers)
Melted Butter, (enough to brush pastry)
2 cups of Fresh Strawberries, cut into quarters
7 oz Honey and 1 oz Scotch – (mix together)
Powered Sugar to sprinkle over each finished piece

Preheat oven to 400°F
Cut 21 Phyllo pastry sheets in half use 3 half sheets of Phyllo for each piece of Cheesecake. As if working on a clock face, lay the first half sheet on the 12 to 6 position, lightly brush with butter, lay the second half sheet on the 2 to 8 position, repeat with Butter, lay the third half on the 10 to 4 position. Place a piece of Cake in the middle and gently pull up all layers of pastry to the top of the cake, 'pinching' to create a 'bundled package'. Lightly brush the top with Butter. Place the wrapped Cheesecake on a baking sheet, lined with parchment paper*. Cover the baking sheet with a simple tent of foil to prevent Cheesecake tops from burning. Bake until pastry is golden brown, approximately 10 minutes. Remove from oven, place cake piece on individual serving plate, drizzle with Scotch-Honey mixture, place several Strawberry pieces on the plate and dust each plate with Powdered Sugar. Now you are ready to serve one the most scrumptious desserts ever!

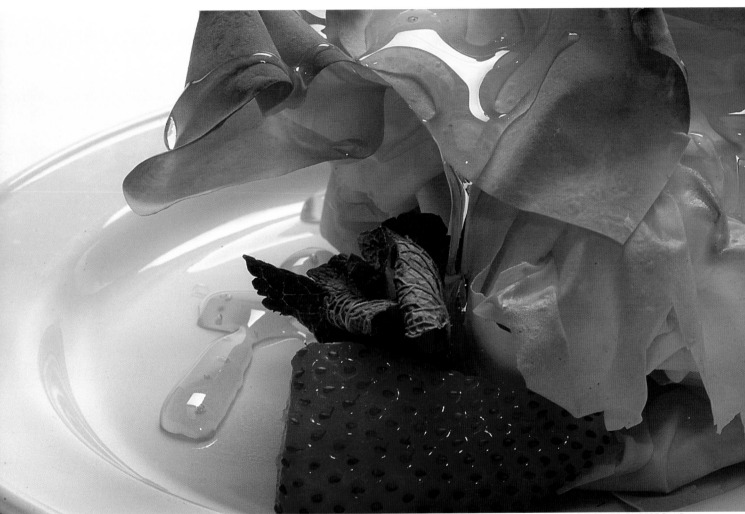

WHITE CHOCOLATE CHEESECAKE

POACHED MERINGUES
WITH BLACKBERRY RHUBARB SAUCE

Would you like to serve an impressive dessert in a hurry? Try these light and airy meringues that are perfect with the fruit sauce. They are a dream to make and heavenly to eat, allowing your guests to float into oblivion!

Serves 6

Sauce

3/4 cup Granulated Sugar
4 cups Rhubarb, diced
4 cups Blackberries
3 Sprigs of Fresh Mint

Meringues

3 cups Milk for Poaching
4 Egg Whites
1/2 cup Granulated Sugar

In a large deep heavy skillet, sprinkle Sugar over the bottom and cook on medium-high heat, watching closely, but not stirring until Sugar melts and turns a golden brown. Carefully pour in Rhubarb, stirring 5-6 minutes or until Rhubarb is tender. Add Blackberries and continue to cook 2 minutes. Remove from heat. Set aside.

In a deep skillet or saucepan, heat Milk, being careful not to boil. In a large bowl, beat Egg Whites until they turn white; slowly add Sugar beating until they are stiff. Drop a rounded tablespoon of Egg White into the Milk; repeat until you have three meringues in the pan. Cook for about 2 minutes, they will swell. (Remember not to let the Milk boil). Remove with a slotted spoon when they "glisten" or do not stick when lightly touched and place on a platter. Repeat until all meringues are cooked. Cool.

To serve, spoon sauce on the serving platter. Place meringues on top, garnish with Mint.

POACHED MERINGUES WITH BLACKBERRY RHUBARB SAUCE

index

index

.index

index

the SHOW

Who's Coming For Dinner, the television cooking show explains the food dilemmas we face everyday with balancing an active lifestyle and of course a 'healthy appetite'.

The show's themes range from making a meal for someone who will only eat meat to the lunch-box dilemma or the treat of breakfast in bed. Jeff assembles menus and recipes that most anyone can prepare at home and enjoy a sense of accomplishment.

Jeff's ability to create delicious, attractive and healthy food is presented in a simple, easy and fun-spirited manner and allows the viewer to recreate their own meals by simply following a few steps.

Jeff's goal is to use ingredients readily available to all, since he too shops at his local market just like his viewing audience.

show

Jeff and Sarah Vogelzang, Dietitian and friend of Jeff, opens our eyes to the endless possibilities of being flexible with menu ideas and fabulous tasting recipes that allow us, the viewer to experience healthy eating with foods that are full of flavour. Jeff says that just because a dish may be lower in fat does not mean you have to sacrifice flavour or taste!

The energy on the show is boosted with the appearance of the "Jon Warren Band", who not only sparks the audience, but seems to get Jeff dancing.

Who's Coming For Dinner is shot in front of a live audience that is brought to life when they smell the tantalizing aromas, see the colourful and beautiful food and of course, sample Jeff's creations.

Be sure to check out Jeff on Who's Coming For Dinner and let his kitchen become part of your kitchen!

Tamara Marcus, Executive Producer